The Politics of Stereotype

Recent Titles in
Contributions in Psychology

The Politics of Stereotype

Psychology and Affirmative Action

Moises F. Salinas

Contributions in Psychology, Number 47
Paul Pedersen, Series Adviser

Westport, Connecticut
London

Library of Congress Cataloging-in-Publication Data

Salinas, Moises F., 1966–
     The politics of stereotype : psychology and affirmative action / Moises
F. Salinas.
          p. cm. — (Contributions in psychology, ISSN 0736-2714; no. 47)
     Includes bibliographical references and index.
     ISBN 0-313-32396-8 (alk. paper)
       1. Discrimination in higher education—United States. 2. Affirmative
action programs—United States. 3. Stereotype (Psychology) I. Title.
II. Series.
     LC212.42.S35   2003
     379.2'6—dc21   2003053637

British Library Cataloguing in Publication Data is available.

Library of Congress Catalog Card Number: 2003053637
ISBN: 0-313-32396-8
ISSN: 0736-2714

First published in 2003

Praeger Publishers, 88 Post Road West, Westport, CT 06881
An imprint of Greenwood Publishing Group, Inc.
www.praeger.com

Printed in the United States of America

I dedicate this book to all the people who have had to overcome hardship because they belong to a group that has been unfairly stigmatized. To all of you I pay my respects.

And to my family—Iky, Danny, Ariela, and Jacky—I love you.

Contents

Series Foreword

Both those who advocate affirmative action and those opposed to affirmative action agree on the importance of "fairness" in the allocation of resources to people. What they disagree on is the definition and measurement of fairness when applied to complex individuals in a complicated society. This condition has led to confusion in the use of the term *affirmative action* and ambiguity in the definition of *fairness criteria*. Political groups and other special interests have taken advantage of this confusion to manipulate others to favor their own special interests for reasons having less to do with fairness and more to do with self-interest

Moises F. Salinas provides in this book the factual information about affirmative action that every psychologist (and others as well) need for their own self-defense as they enter into arguments about what is and what is not fair. The purpose of this book is first to explore how the issue of affirmative action became so confusing by reviewing the historical development of the term. Second, this book will propose a positive course of action based on psychological data about the role of diversity and individual differences in society. This book will enable the reader toward informed debate of a complicated but extremely important social issue in our multicultural society.

The intent of legislation to support affirmative action has always attempted to support the fair treatment of all people in our society. The absence of a level playing field and the existence of privilege among those with the most power has in this case, as in the role of government generally, required the regulation of public behavior to increase the likelihood of fairness. This, in turn, has restrained those who are most powerful and most advantaged in ways that they have found objectionable. Legislating fairness is never easy and is always inadequate, but inevitably necessary. There are four types of affirmative action programs addressed in this book: (1) recruiting qualified women and minorities; (2) eliminating programs, policies, or obstacles that prevent women and minorities from mistreatment; (3) providing "soft" preferential treatment to some groups; and (4) providing "hard" preferential treatment to other individuals. Each program has its own strengths and weaknesses.

The five "myths" surrounding affirmative action are particularly interesting. Each myth is matched with hard data that challenges that myth's validity. The psychological research on affirmative action has generally supported attempts to create fairness while at the same time documenting the inadequacies of some programs more than others. The politics of stereotypes provides still another valuable perspective to the reader about those attempting to use this ambiguous issue for their own interests.

In the final chapter, Salinas frames a proposal for a "learner-centered" paradigm that might be more adequate than other educational programs in providing fairness and addressing the problems of affirmative action. There is no simple solution to this complex problem and Salinas does not minimize the difficulty of creating a fair society. However, in his positive program, Salinas does provide valuable ideas to start us going in the right direction.

This book fits with the other books in the "Contributions to Psychology" series in describing how psychology serves society. The many books in this series define the cutting edge of psychology as it is applied to social issues. Each book has focused on a specific issue of importance, providing building blocks to those who deliver psychological services in our society. It is with great pride that we welcome this most recent contribution to the series.

Paul Pedersen
Department of Psychology
University of Hawaii
Series Adviser

Acknowledgments

The completion of a book is very seldom the work of a single person. Either directly, or indirectly, every academic piece is only the continuation, and hopefully the preface, of the work of many others who have contributed to the field. It is also the product of many individuals, from research assistants to copy editors to family members, without whom the burden of writing a book would be too much for a single author. Therefore, I would like to begin this book by thanking a great number of people who helped me and supported me in this project. My research assistants—Maureen Walton, Irene Biros, and James Bendezu—who worked really hard compiling materials and checking references. My colleagues—Carol Austad, Bob Stowe, Nicole Amador, and Hillary Lipka—who helped review and revise the first drafts of the manuscript and who made great suggestions. To my colleague Scott Plous, who early on made some great suggestions that helped me focus the purpose of this book, and to all the researchers before me who produced and published the fantastic body of evidence regarding affirmative action, psychology, and education that is the basis for this work. To all of you, my most sincere thanks. Finally, to my family, who has endured this process with me and has sacrificed many hours that would have been spent playing in the backyard or sharing a dinner together to support me in this project. Thank you for your support, your encouragement, and your understanding.

Introduction

Not long ago, I received a phone call (in fact, about a half dozen phone calls) from a person calling from the University of Connecticut, who was very insistent in asking me some questions for a survey he was conducting. Assuming (wrongly) that he was a student collecting data for a serious research project, I was finally able to speak with him for a few minutes after his sixth or seventh call to answer his questionnaire. What followed took me completely by surprise. The questioner proceeded to ask me if I supported granting preferential treatment in the hiring or admissions of people to the university, based on race or gender. My answer to that specific question was, of course, no. By definition, no one should be granted preferential treatment (which implies partiality) on the basis of anything. I suspected, however, that that was not what he was trying to get at and, therefore, still thinking I was speaking to a misguided student, I explained to him that the question he was asking was prone to bias, and therefore not a valid one. At that point, he thanked me and hung up and that was the end of it. Or was it?

In fact, a few weeks later, I discovered that the survey was actually sponsored by an antiaffirmative action group, and that the results of this survey were misrepresented in the media as proving that most faculty in Connecticut public universities *opposed* affirmative action.

The reason this story is relevant for this book is not because of the results of the survey, but because it exemplifies one of the most widely held misconceptions about affirmative action: that it is a system to simply give certain groups some "preference" over others. Affirmative action is not a system of granting preference to anyone. Nor is it a system of "quotas" designed to ensure equal representation of different groups in the basis of ethnicity or gender. Furthermore, affirmative action is not "reparation" for previous discrimination, as some of its critics tend to argue, for example, for how long do we have to pay reparation to African Americans for slavery, to women for ages of discrimination. Affirmative action, at its core, recognizes that for some groups in America certain inequalities have existed, and continue to exist, that make it difficult for us to be a true meritocracy. By providing equal access and opportunity to resources to certain groups, affirmative action is an attempt to "correct" that inherent bias, not at its root causes, but by giving members of the disadvantaged groups a "boost" when they apply for admission or employment. In other words, affirmative action compensates for the disadvantaged "at the top," after a long educational and socialization process, instead of fixing it "at the bottom," right from the beginning when intervention is more likely to be succesful.

Let me give you an example of what I mean by these inherent inequalities. A Mexican American child is born in the United States to immigrant parents. She is already disadvantaged because of language issues (English is probably not spoken at home, or if spoken, is probably only at a basic conversational level) and the limited education of her parents (they very likely never completed more than a few years of elementary education, if at all). In addition, low socioeconomic status forces her parents to work double shifts depriving the child of a stimulating environment at home. OK, so far, that is sad, but definitely not the result of anything America did at the social or political level. But it does not stop there. The child will probably attend a poor school district, that has large student–teacher ratios, limited educational resources (for example, computers), and few extracurricular activities or advanced placement classes. The notion behind affirmative action is thus the following: If this child had equal opportunity and access to resources, her performance (in, by the way, an arbitrary and problematic set of criteria, like standardized academic tests) would have been relatively higher. Let us, then, correct for that deficit at "the top," when this child has to be compared to and selected against other persons who do not share this deficit (for example, employment application or admissions to higher education). In other words, let us take affirmative action to compensate for that inherent social deficit that is not the fault of the individual but the result of social and economic circumstances (how these circumstances came to be and why they are, at least partially, the result of American political decisions and cultural patterns will be discussed in Chapter 1).

There is, however, a problem with attempting to remedy for these inequalities at the top. While it was clear both from landmark desegregation cases (for example, *Brown et al. v. Board of Education of Topeka et al.*, 349 US 294 [1955]) and affirmative action legislation that an immediate, drastic solution was required, affirmative action attempted to correct for this deficit *only* at the top. This approach was, and still is, not only relatively successful but, given that most of these inequalities still exist today (although some of the groups might be slightly different), is necessary and essential. Affirmative action, however, was never meant to stop there, an after-the-fact correction, yet it somehow did. Affirmative action was meant to end the inequalities at the bottom, at the root. Affirmative action was supposed to ensure that all children had equal educational opportunity and access to resources. That all children, regardless of race, gender or socioeconomic status had the chance to receive an education in good schools that are not overcrowded and that provide them with the latest resources and extracurricular opportunities. Furthermore, affirmative action was supposed to ensure that children coming from disadvantaged groups had community resources to at least minimize, if not make up for, the impact that having low socioeconomic status in addition to parents who work multiple shifts, or in many cases broken families, would have on their potential. If forty years ago affirmative action had not stopped "correcting" the deficits at the top, but instead fixed the inequalities at the bottom, perhaps affirmative action would have become obsolete and died of its own weight, and we would not be debating this subject because children from disadvantaged groups would not be disadvantaged, and therefore there would be no need to correct anything. It did not. And until it does, there will still be a need for affirmative action as we know it today. In the long run, however, the goal of all of us who support affirmative action is to make it obsolete by ending the inequalities.

The purpose of this book, therefore, is twofold. First, it will explore how we got to where we are. It will address such questions as

What is the history of affirmative action? Why did it fail to end inequalities at their root? How do stereotypes and prejudice not only shape the current debate on affirmative action, but also impact political and social decisions that affect disadvantaged groups in our society? Second, it will propose a course of action. By presenting what psychology and education have learned over the years about the value of diversity and individual differences, and the inequalities that are still prevalent today, we will lay the foundation for a rational course of action to solve some of the most pressing issues. Finally, while I recognize that this book will hardly be the last word on this controversial subject, it is my hope that it will bring to the table some ideas that will influence future discourse on this issue—discourse that will be less plagued by stereotypes, myths, and preconceptions.

Chapter 1

What Is Affirmative Action?

The Origins of Affirmative Action

In 1995, President Bill Clinton created a commission to undertake the first comprehensive review of affirmative action policy and to make recommendations about its future direction. In section 1, the report plainly states that affirmative action enjoys no clear and widely shared definition, and that this lack of definition contributes to the confusion and miscommunication surrounding the issue (White House, 1995). In other words, there is wide disagreement on what affirmative action really is. This problem has been the hallmark of affirmative action from the beginning. It originated from the vague language that was used in the executive orders that gave birth to affirmative action in the first place (Skrentny, 1996). Traditionally, the birth of the term *affirmative action* can be traced to Executive Order 10925 (1961). Under the influence of the nascent civil rights movements, and aware of the still rampant discrimination that occurred all throughout the United States, John F. Kennedy established the Committee on Equal Employment Opportunity a few weeks after assuming the presidency. Its goal was to end discrimination in employment by the federal government and its contractors. The language of this order required federal contracts to

not discriminate against any employee or applicant for employment because of race, creed, color, or national origin. The Contractor will take affirmative action, to ensure that applicants are employed, and that employees are treated during employment, without regard to their race, creed, color, or national origin. (p. 1)

In fact, this executive order is not only vague in terms of the definition of affirmative action, but it also fails to elaborate on how the contractors are supposed to achieve this goal. Furthermore, this original order does not require that any federal contractor or agency actually implement any programs to achieve equal employment, it merely requires them to treat applicants "without regard to their race, creed, color, or national origin." As a result, this definition has been interpreted both academically (Wilson, 1998) and legally (*Hopwood v. State of Texas*, 84 F.3d 720, 722–24 [5th Cir. 1996]) as merely requiring a "blind" hiring process in which essentially it was forbidden to take race and ethnicity into account.

Some commentators (Cahn, 1995; Wilson, 1998) have suggested that President Lyndon B. Johnson was aware of the shortcomings of this order and therefore issued a revised Executive Order 11246 (1963), which stated the following:

It is the policy of the government of the United States to provide equal opportunity in federal employment for all qualified persons, to prohibit discrimination in employment because of race, creed, color or national origin, and to promote the full realization of equal employment opportunity through a positive, continuing program in each department and agency. (p. 1)

In other words, Johnson not only required from the federal government and its contractors to have a "race-blind" hiring process, but also to have an active program to seek and recruit qualified minorities for their ranks. Although this new order was an improvement in terms of spelling out what was expected of employers, it still was quite ambiguous when it came to the specific components that defined a program as one supporting affirmative action.

An Evolving Definition

It was not until the next decade, during the Nixon administration, that the U.S. Department of Labor (U.S. Department of Labor [USDOL], 1971) attempted to clarify what an affirmative action program was supposed to look like. It issued an order explaining to employers that an affirmative action program should include:

A. An analysis of areas within which the contractor is deficient in the utilization of minority groups and women.
B. Goals and timetables to which the contractor's good faith efforts must be directed to correct the deficiencies.
C. Pursuant to the language of the original executive orders, the goals were not supposed to be specific quotas, but "targets reasonably attainable by means of applying every good faith effort to make all aspects of the entire affirmative action program work." (p. 3)

The USDOL order was quite controversial. It essentially directed employers to *take race into account* (how else are you supposed to analyze and solve the deficiency in utilization of minorities?), contradicting the original language of Executive Orders 10925 and 11246. In addition, it plainly told employers they were expected to have a certain reasonable percentage of minorities working for them. The government did not care how they accomplished this goal as long as they did not use quotas. In other words, it obligated federal agencies and contractors to hire a percentage of minorities, but this goal was not supposed to happen in the most logical way of achieving it. Once again affirmative action was defined in terms of what is not (quotas) instead of what was supposed to be.

The frustration with the definition of affirmative action is further reflected in the report of the comprehensive review undertaken by the Clinton administration in 1995 (White House, 1995). They attempted to agree on a working definition that could be useful for the purposes of analyzing the effects of affirmative action:

For purposes of this review, "affirmative action" is any effort taken to expand opportunity for women or racial, ethnic and national origin minorities by using membership in those groups that have been subject to discrimination as a consideration. Measures adopted in court orders or consent decrees, however, were outside the scope of the Review. (p. 27)

Although this working definition is adequate for the study of affirmative action, it lacks sufficient specificity to guide an employer or educational institution attempting to implement a program to increase the representation of minorities. However, the White House report suggests a number of guidelines, based on a Supreme Court decision in the case of *Adarand Constructors, Inc. v. Peña*, 515 US 200 (1995), to develop affirmative action programs that are "fair." Once more the emphasis is on what should not be done instead of what should:

1. Should avoid the use of quotas;
2. Should consider other, "race neutral" options;
3. Should not be rigid;
4. Should be limited in time;
5. Should not unduly burden the non-beneficiaries.

To make matters more confusing, it is important to note, as I will discuss later, that even in the case of some affirmative action programs that *do* follow these guidelines, the federal court has found that these programs unconstitutionally discriminate against nonbeneficiaries (for example, *Hopwood v. State of Texas*, 84 F.3d 720, 722–24 [5th 1996]).

The most significant Supreme Court case directly affecting university admissions, however, was the 1978 decision on the *Regents of the Univ. of Cal. v. Bakke*, 438 US 265 (1978). In this case, White male medical school applicant Allan Bakke sued the University of California–Davis after his application to medical school was rejected in spite of relative good scores. Bakke claimed it was a case of discrimination and that his constitutional equal protection rights had been violated by the university's affirmative action policy. This policy reserved sixteen spaces of a total of one hundred for minority applicants. According to Rubio (2001) the university adopted this policy in 1971, after the 1968 class contained no African Americans, Hispanics, or Native Americans. The case eventually made it to the Supreme Court, where, by a split vote of 5 to 4, the Court issued an opinion that is "widely viewed as an intellectual muddle but a pragmatic triumph" (Parloff, 2002, p. 122). In this ruling, Justice Lewis Powell, writing for the majority, argues that while specific quotas are indeed unconstitutional, diversity is a legitimate goal universities can seek, and therefore taking into account race as just one in a series of factors to make admissions decisions was permissible. The full Court decision, however, as much else in the affirmative action debate, remained unclear regarding the how and when would taking race into account be permissible.

In summary, the legal definition of affirmative action is, to this date, unclear, confusing, and, at best, a work in progress that continues to be shaped after almost forty years by the courts and the legislation.

Beyond the Legal Points

If the lack of a concrete definition is problematic from the strictly legal point of view, that is not necessarily true for the political and social realms. Different groups have seen affirmative action as an opportunity to advance their own agendas and to shape American culture and society, and have therefore offered their own very concrete and clear definitions and interpretations of affirmative action.

Supporters of affirmative action tend to see beyond the legal issues and more into matters of social justice, equal opportunity, and reparation. For instance, in 1995, Jesse Jackson, leader of the Rainbow Coalition, defined affirmative action as a remedy to "repair the effects of past and *present* discrimination. It creates equal opportunities for people who have been historically and currently discriminated against" (p. 10). Similarly, Marcia Greenberger (1995), founder of the National Women's Law Center, looks at affirmative action as a mechanism to compensate for inherent social bias and injustice. Although she differentiates between affirmative action in employment, education, and business ownership, the common element of her definition is the use of programs to eliminate underrepresentation of qualified people from certain groups, in areas where their participation has been discouraged.

On the other hand, critics of affirmative action (for example, Carter, 1993; Steele, 1998) see it as a system of preference, in which some people who are "less qualified" get some extra points because of race. At best, they point out, is a system which assumes that the best minority candidates are not as good as the best nonminority ones, and therefore the system is not only unfair, but damaging since it perpetuates the negative intellectual stereotype of minorities (see, for example, Heilman, Block, & Lucas, 1992; Summers, 1991). At its extreme, the criticism of affirmative action sees it as reverse discrimination and an attack to a most valued American institution: the meritocracy (Ingraham, 1995; Puddington, 1995).

Which brings us back to the issue of merit. Merit is supposed to relate to a quality, a demonstration of ability or achievement. But like any other qualitative judgment, quality is not only contingent on the subjective judgment of the observer, but totally dependent on context. The problem is that in the United States, we are attempting to combine a subjective and contextual (soft) concept like merit with our obsession for objective (hard) measures, resulting in a system that is at best flawed and at worst biased (Kohn, 2000). In fact, research has found that when we make admission and employment decisions giving heavier weight to complex, qualitative examples of achievement like interviews and essays and less weight to "objective" measures like standardized tests (especially standardized tests), minority representation both in employment and education automatically increases, even if race or ethnicity is not used as a factor (see, for example, Edwards, Maldonado, & Calvin, 1999; Sigelman, 1997)

In educational admissions, merit tends to be defined by far as scores on standardized tests. These tests are popular because they are largely perceived to be objective and an economical way to make admissions decisions for the hundreds of thousands of applications that colleges get every year. However, and regardless of the controversy regarding the issue of test bias that is still very much under debate (see, for example, Jencks & Phillips, 1998; Valencia & Salinas, 2000), are these tests really an objective measure of merit? Indeed if we look to merit as achievement over time, which is a *process*, then a single numerical score (even assuming it is psychometrically unbiased), which is an indicator of *outcome*, cannot be a comprehensive and valid measure of merit. In other words, admissions tests might (or might not) be good predictors of future scholastic and professional potential, but at no point did their creators attempt to make them an indicator of merit when defined as achievement. (Keep in mind that even the predictive value of admissions tests in professional programs like law or medicine is limited, since they usually are not very good predictors of professional examination results like the legal bar exams or the medical boards [see, for example, Basco, Gilbert, Chessman, & Blue, 2000; Kidder, 2001; Kulatunga-Moruzi & Norman, 2002; Webb, Waugh, & Herbert, 1993; Wightman, 1997]).

Furthermore, employers have little information to judge merit when they hire new graduates from our colleges and universities. Under those circumstances, the college of attendance (for example, Harvard versus Podunk State University) becomes a major factor in determining merit. But if the admissions process to selective universities was tainted in the first place by systematic error, using the school of attendance as an indicator of merit would only compound such an error.

To measure process in psychology or education, we know that we cannot rely on a single test score. In fact, we have to use a pretest–posttest design in which the subjects are tested before (as a starting point) and then after any program. For example, we watch two groups of swimmers in a competition that went to different swimming improvement programs. After a single competition, there is no doubt that swimmers from group A are much faster than the ones from group B. But if we want to know how much improvement there was for two different groups of swimming students, we have to watch them swim before the program, and then after the program (after all, swimmers from group A could have been faster from the beginning than swimmers from group B). Absent the possibility of a pretest, we use a process called "analysis of covariance" (see, for example, Agresti & Finlay, 1997). In this process, we have to identify some indicators of preexisting differences (like records from previous swimming competitions) and statistically use them to control for these differences. If we want to evaluate the students on their real merits, we have to make an assumption: What if this program had started with swimmers in both groups that were at the exact same level? In other words, we level the playing field so we can be sure that the differences observed are due to the achievement in the program and not to preexisting differences. Now, let us take our analogy and move it to the realm of race and testing. If we have two ethnic groups coming out of high school, and we want to determine which group has achieved the most, and is therefore more "meritorious," we have to know where they started from, not just where they ended up. After all, one group could have started at the top of a hypothetical scale of learning and just cruise through school making only marginal gains. At the same time, the second group could have started at the bottom of our hypothetical scale, but managed to improve tremendously and get to three-quarters of the way to the top (see Figure 1.1).

Looking at the groups just at the end would surely tell you that the first group is better than the second. But if we look at the process, which one is really more meritorious? Which one is more deserving of praise, and has achieved the most? If we were to compare their scores

Figure 1.1

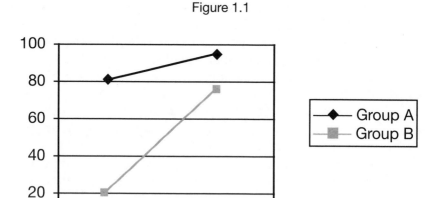

using an analysis of covariance, we would see that the second group actually scored a lot higher than the first.

In a sense, affirmative action is attempting to achieve the same result as an analysis of covariance. It attempts to take into account pre-existing differences in access to resources, educational opportunities, socioeconomic status, and a lot of other social and cultural factors. It has to make an assumption: What if minority groups and women had had the same access and resources as White males? Unless you believe that there are biological differences in intelligence and ability (see, for example, Herrnstein & Murray, 1996; Jensen, 1998), the logical conclusion is that their representation at the top colleges and higher management should be very similar to their percentage in the population. Affirmative action, therefore, can be defined in this vein merely as an attempt to correct the systematic error that exists in our subjective evaluation of merit.

Ideally, however, as I will discuss later, even the more tenacious supporters of affirmative action would agree that it is better to correct the differences at the beginning, to make affirmative action obsolete because it is not needed anymore (see, for example, Kahlenberg, 1997; Patterson, 1998; Rhode, 1997). In other words, instead of compensating for an uneven playing field when decisions for employment or admission are made, really level the playing field and provide equal resources and access to minorities.

More Than One Affirmative Action

As we have seen, the legal definition of affirmative action is complex, confusing, and a work in progress that keeps being interpreted by the courts and the political machinery. One possibility is that this confusion arises in part from the fact that affirmative action is not one but a number of different things that are covered under one umbrella term, but which in fact are relatively different. Sure enough, in the psychological literature, four different types of affirmative action programs have been identified (see, for example, Doverspike, Taylor, & Winfred, 2000; Ledvinka & Scarpello, 1991):

1. Attempting to increase recruiting of qualified women and minorities.
2. Eliminating programs, policies, or other obstacles that prevent minorities or women from being accepted, hired, or promoted.
3. Granting the member of the minority group "soft" preferential treatment. In other words, when minority and majority applicants are equally qualified, use group membership as a deciding factor.
4. Granting the member of the minority group "hard" preferential treatment. This means that a member of the minority group is selected because group membership is taken into account as a major consideration.

The first two types of affirmative action programs are the least controversial. The fourth type, although very controversial, is very seldom seen today because it is the one type that the courts are most likely (and have most often) declared unconstitutional. The third type, however, is the type of affirmative action program that is generating the most polemic since it hovers at the edge of the programs that are clearly permissible under the law and the ones that are probably not. To gain a better understanding of these four types of programs, let us revisit some examples of each as they would relate, for instance, to university admissions.

Recruitment

State University A has decided to increase its budget in order to recruit qualified minorities. As a result, the office of diversity and retention puts together a plan. They will increase the number of recruiters that will go to high schools in underprivileged areas with high concentrations of African American and Hispanic students, and look for potential applicants. In addition, they will develop promotional materials in Spanish and some that feature minorities and minority-oriented services more prominently. Also, they will advertise the university in newspapers and magazines that cater specifically to minorities. Their goal is to increase the number of qualified minority applicants by 20 percent.

Removal of Barriers

University of B is widely known and has good name recognition among minority populations in its state. However, and even though they get a fair amount of applications from minority students, every year they accept a percentage that is well bellow the proportional number of statewide high school graduates. University of B decided to conduct a study to determine why minorities are not applying. They discovered a number of issues:

- Their admission policies, which give preference to children of alumni (most of which tended to be White and middle-upper class), hinders minority students from being accepted.
- A weighting system that considered the ranking of the high school in the state, as well as a student's grades, as part of the calculation for admission, tended to benefit students from mostly suburban, White areas.
- Most important, the heavy reliance on the use of a standardized test for admission decisions benefited Whites, who tended to score higher on the test than minorities.

As a result of the study, University of B is now considering moving away from their current admissions system and granting automatic admission to every high school graduate in the state who is in the top 5 percent of their class.

"Soft" Preferential Treatment

C Institute of Technology, a state institution that offers degrees mostly in engineering-related fields, has a student body that is 88 percent male. Although for years they have had an aggressive recruiting program aimed at qualified females, their percentage of female students still falls way short of long-term institutional objectives. As a result, the institute has decided to implement a new affirmative action policy: when a female and male applicant have otherwise substantially similar qualifications, preference should be given to the female applicant. Furthermore, it is clear from the way the policy is written that the admission test score and the grade point average (GPA) can be considered "substantially similar" even if there is a small difference of a few percentage points, which could lead to the possibility that a male applicant with a slightly higher score would be rejected in favor of a female applicant.

"Hard" Preferential Treatment

D College has a firm commitment to increase the percentage of underprivileged groups admitted to the school. To achieve its institutional goals, the college decides to set specific percentages of the protected groups that should be admitted every semester. Accordingly, it is decided that 50 percent of admissions must be females, while 20 percent must be ethnic minorities. To accomplish this, it is decided to have separate "pools" of applicants, and the top students from each pool will be admitted until the desired percentage of admission is achieved. Applicants from different pools, therefore, will not be compared to each other in their qualifications but only to other applicants in their pool.

As you can see, some of the confusion arising from the affirmative action debate derives from the fact that affirmative action is not one but at least four different types of programs. One of the gravest methodological mistakes we make when conducting research and opinion polls regarding affirmative action is the failure to clearly define what type of affirmative action we are talking about. As I will discuss in subsequent chapters, it is likely that very different reactions will be obtained when the interviewer assumes (or the poll suggests) that affirmative action refers to "hard" preferential treatment (as, by the way, was the case of Proposition 209 in California), or when the poll is worded so it reflects any of the first three types of affirmative action programs.

Political Movement

In the past few years, changes in policy, legislation, and the legal system have altered both the definition of affirmative action and the ways in which it is implemented. The first case to challenge affirmative action since the 1978 Supreme Court *Regents of the Univ. of Cal. v. Bakke* ruling was the case of *Hopwood v. State of Texas*. In 1992, Cheryl Hopwood, claiming she was discriminated against when denied admission because of her race, sued the University of Texas Law School. In this case, the Fifth Circuit Court of Appeals ruled, contrary to Bakke, that diversity in education was not necessarily a compelling interest for the state and therefore the university must eliminate its use of ethnic factors in admissions. The State of Texas appealed this decision to the Supreme Court, but in 1996, the review of this case was denied and all requests for further proceedings were rejected.

With this decision, the State of Texas was effectively prevented from seeking any further appeals, eliminating since then all affirmative action admissions policies at its public universities. This had an immediate effect on the racial diversity of the university system in Texas. For example, data released in 2000 by the University of Texas School of Law (www.utexas.edu) shows that after the Supreme Court decision to deny review of Hopwood in 1996, enrollment of African American students dropped to about 10 percent of previous levels.

As a result, in 1997 the Texas legislature adopted a resolution automatically awarding spots in any Texas public university to the top 10 percent of all the state's high school classes. That policy had the effect of increasing minority representation to levels similar to those before the Hopwood case. But the policy is still problematic, not only because it does not apply to graduate or professional programs, but because the only reason this solution works is that Texas's "public schools are still de facto segregated, because housing patterns are de facto segregated" (Parloff, 2002). When this is the case, the top 10 percent of a mostly Latino high school will most probably be Hispanic.

The second major milestone that has affected how affirmative action is viewed and implemented, occurred in parallel in California, and culminated with the referendum to approve Proposition 209, which banned all California state agencies from using race or sex as a hiring factor.

The story began very quietly when a member of the University of California Board of Regents, Ward Connerly, proposed to end considering race as a factor in hiring, contracting, and admitting at the University of California System. The proposal sparked a furious debate that spread all throughout California and the rest of the nation, since a vote that would effectively end affirmative action in the largest public higher education system in the United States,would have been the most dramatic scaling back of these initiatives since they were instituted. Finally, in July 1995, the Board of Regents, by a vote of 15 to 10, and after weeks of fiery debate that ended up in a bizarre day of protests, speeches, and even an evacuation of the meeting due to a bomb threat (Lively, 1995), decided to end all race-based hiring and admissions programs at the University of California System.

As significant as this decision might have seemed, it was, actually, just the beginning of a comprehensive campaign by antiaffirmative action supporters in California. In fact, the controversial decision by the Board of Regents regarding admissions never had a chance to be implemented because Proposition 209 kicked in before the date the Board's decision was supposed to take effect. According to Douglass (1998), there were suspicions that

Regent Ward Connerly and Governor and Regent Pete Wilson were using the university for political purposes—as a vehicle to generate publicity and support for a proposed state constitutional amendment to ban race and gender decision making in public agencies (Proposition 209), to launch a national campaign against affirmative action, and to bolster Governor Wilson's presidential campaign. (p. 943)

Sure enough, just as the Board of Regents' proposal was being debated all around California, Glynn Custred and Tom Wood, two professors in the California public higher education system, were busy working on Proposition 209, or as supporters called it the "California Civil Rights Initiative."

The Web site of the California Secretary of State (1996) presents the following official summary of Proposition 209:

- Prohibits the state, local governments, districts, public universities, colleges, and schools, and other government instrumentalities from discriminating against or giving preferential treatment to any individual

or group in public employment, public education, or public contracting on the basis of race, sex, color, ethnicity, or national origin.
- Does not prohibit reasonably necessary, bona fide qualifications based on sex and actions necessary for receipt of federal funds.
- Mandates enforcement to extent permitted by federal law.
- Requires uniform remedies for violations.
- Provides for severability of provisions if invalid.

According to Eastland (1996), Custred and Wood's plan, supported by Connerly, was to get the California legislature to place the bill on the March 1996 state ballot. That, however, required a vote in the largely Democratic legislature, a quite difficult task that faced severe opposition by the party leadership. And sure enough, Assembly Speaker Willie Brown blocked the vote, and forced Wood, Custred, and Connerly to take advantage of a California constitutional provision that allows them to put the measure directly on the ballot by gathering 750,000 signatures. They collected the necessary signatures, and placed Proposition 209 on the November 1996 ballot.

Finally, on November 5, California voters approved the measure by a vote of 54 to 46 percent, a margin that although quite smaller than most polls had predicted just a few weeks before the vote, was still enough to approve the measure and become Article I, Section 31 of the California Constitution.

The day after, the American Civil Liberties Union and other legal advocacy groups filed a lawsuit in U.S. District Court alleging that Proposition 209 violated the Equal Protection Clause of the Fourteenth Amendment of the U.S. Constitution. Two weeks later, the presiding judge, Thelton Henderson, granted a preliminary injunction against Proposition 209. However, by April 1997, the Ninth Circuit Court of Appeals vacated the preliminary injunction, and finally, in November 1997, the U.S. Supreme Court killed any other avenues for appeal by declining to hear the case.

The effects of these two parallel developments were immediate and startling. For example, many minority students decided not to even bother applying to elite state colleges in the affected states. The Times Higher Education Supplement (Cornwell, 1997) reported that "[t]he numbers of minority students applying to state colleges in Texas and California have dropped sharply" (p. 9). One year later, the consequences could be fully seen. According to Cornwell (1998), the number of African American freshmen admitted by the University of California–Berkeley (UC–Berkeley) declined from 562 in 1997 to 191 in 1998,and the number of Latino students fell, amazingly, from 1,266 to 60.

Other numbers are equally dramatic. According to Reibstein (1998) the number of admissions offered to African American applicants at the University of California's three law schools declined, after Proposition 209, from over two hundred to just fifty-nine, and only sixteen of them decided to attend. At UC–Berkeley the 1997 first-year law school class had only one African American student. Reibstein (1998) reports a similar situation in Texas after *Hopwood*. Only four African American students enrolled at the University of Texas Law School in 1997 compared to twenty-nine in 1996.

While the initial refusal of the U.S. Supreme Court to review either the *Hopwood* decision or the constitutionality of Proposition 209 seemed to be consistent with a larger trend to eliminate affirmative action, the recent case of the University of Michigan has forced the Court into a situation in which it can no longer ignore the issue.

The case that seems to have brought the trend against affirmative action to a pause is *Gratz v. Bollinger*, 122 F. Supp. 2d 811 (E.D. Mich. 2000). Jennifer Gratz, a woman from a Detroit working-class family, applied in 1995 to the University of Michigan at Ann Arbor. She had strong, although not exceptional, credentials (a 3.7 GPA, and a score on the American College Test just under the nintieth percentile, according to Reibstein, 1998). She was denied admission to Ann Arbor, although she later enrolled in the less prestigious University of Michigan's Dearborn campus. She filed suit against the university, but in December 2000, a federal judge in Detroit ruled against her by upholding the university's affirmative action policy.

In May 2002, a divided Sixth Circuit ruled 5 to 4 that the University of Michigan admissions policy is allowed under the Constitution. Following Judge Powell's reasoning in *Bakke*, the court concluded that the policy was permissible since the school needs it to maintain an educationally diverse environment.

Although consistent with *Bakke*, this latest decision by the Sixth Circuit Court of Appeals seems to be directly in conflict with the *Hopwood* ruling by the Fifth Circuit and the Proposition 209 ruling by the Ninth Circuit courts. Most experts agree that this is a constitutionally complicated position the Supreme Court will have no option but to resolve. However, the fact that the affirmative action issue seems finally to be heading toward the Supreme Courts themselves, the signs are not encouraging for supporters of affirmative action. According to Schrag (1997), the U.S. Supreme Court has shown a clear bias toward not upholding any pro-affirmative action–related policy. In addition to declining or deferring review of the *Hopwood* case and Proposition 209, the court has severely limited the consideration of ethnicity in federal contracting (for example, *Adarand v. Peña*), it precluded the use of race as a factor in drawing congressional and legislative districts (*Shaw v. Hunt*, 116 S.Ct. 1894, 135 L.Ed.2d 207 [1996]), and it declined to review the *Kirwin v. Podberesky*, 38 F.3d 147 (4th Cir. 1994) Fourth Circuit Court of Appeals decision doing away with a University of Maryland scholarship program for minorities. It is highly possible that by the time this book is in press or shortly thereafter, a divided Supreme Court will reverse itself, repealing *Bakke* and terminating once and for all affirmative action in college admissions as we have known it for thirty years.

A Look at the Alternatives

As both court rulings and new legislation place increased limits on the use of affirmative action, new programs have emerged that are attempting to increase minority representation without running afoul of the law. Texas and California, as the first states to have been severely limited in the use of affirmative action and as two of the largest states in the nation, can be viewed as examples of the shape of things to come. In both cases, the strategy has been to reduce or eliminate the relative weight of quantitative measures that show a noticeable gap in performance between minorities and nonminorities, specifically the SAT (née Scholastic Aptitude Test), and to increase or add other factors to the decision-making process.

As I have mentioned, after losing the *Hopwood* case, Texas implemented the controversial "10 Percent Rule." The concept is a simple one, and at face value, it appears to be completely race neutral: State colleges would automatically grant admission to any student whose GPA was in the top 10 percent of his or her high school class. Thus, top state universities were allowed to take minority students who stand out in low-performing schools, and who would not have made the cut under the previous non–affirmative action acceptance policy.

However, in addition to criticism I have discussed from affirmative action supporters, this policy has also been criticized by opponents of affirmative action (see Merritt, 2002) who challenge that even if the policy is race neutral at face value, it would still be unconstitutional if its intent was racial.

California is adopting a different, more sophisticated approach. In that state, the legislature mandates the University of California System to accept the top 12.5 percent of high school graduates every year. Unlike the new Texas system, however, which is based solely on GPA, to select the students, the university requires undergraduate prospects to succeed on a number of predetermined courses and to take the SAT I.

Before proceeding, let me provide some history on the SAT. Created in 1926, the SAT, or Scholastic Aptitude Test at the time (the acronym's meaning has since been discontinued by The College Board, publishers of the SAT), was designed to measure "aptitude," which is supposed to be an innate mental ability, as opposed to "achievement." According to Gose and Selingo (2001), it became popular in the 1940s and 1950s as top university officials looked for alternatives to traditional achievement tests, which favored upper-class students who could attend high-quality, private schools. At the time, with IQ tests at the zenith of their popularity, the SAT, was seen as a fairer, more "scientific" alternative that would allow top universities to select their students based on objective aptitude measures rather than family connections (Lemann, 1999). Although the SAT (later renamed the SAT I with the introduction of the SAT II) is still a solid test that has been thoroughly researched and supported, since its beginnings, it has been greatly criticized as being biased against minorities, having only modest predictive value regarding student success, and, mostly, being too closely correlated to socioeconomic status (see, for example, Lawlor, Richman, & Richman, 1997; Lynn & Mau, 2001; Schmitt & Dorans, 1991; Vars & Bowen, 1998).

In addition to grades and the SAT I, applicants to the University of California also have to take three SAT IIs. Unlike the SAT I, the SAT II is a subject-specific "achievement" test. All of these factors are combined to make admissions decisions.

One of the reasons the SAT became a popular method of student selection was because of its predictive value regarding student success at the college level. However, according to Gose and Selingo (2001) the University of California's data suggests that their formula combining the SAT I, the SAT II, and GPA has no better predictive value regarding how a student will do academically when compared to a formula using only grades and the SAT II. As a result, University of California President Richard Atkinson, a well-known cognitive psychologist, and former director of the National Science Foundation, proposed sweeping changes to the admissions process that sparked a national controversy.

The first part of Atkinson's proposal was fairly simple: keep the SAT II and use a new version of the SAT I that would be more achievement oriented. The adoption of this policy by the University of California has already prompted The College Board to begin the development of this new SAT test that is not only more achievement oriented but it is based mostly on high school curriculum material.

However, the second part of Atkinson's plan was a lot more controversial. In addition to the quantitative measures, the University of California will implement a process of "comprehensive review." This is a holistic admissions process that is used in some elite universities and many graduate programs, under which the entire record of every student is taken into account, including factors such as handicaps overcome, achievements, talents, special skills, and diversity of background, therefore reducing the reliance on quantitative measures.

The comprehensive review policy was adopted by the Board of Regents of the University of California in 2001, and although the data will not be available until late in 2002, it is already expected to significantly increase minority representation.

Adjusting Bias: Psychometric Methods

Psychological research in affirmative action has also looked at other psychometrically (if not politically) feasible ways of achieving a more balanced ethnic representation, by reducing some of the performance gap that exists in current instruments used for selection and admission. In theory, the advantage of psychometric methods is that they are rooted in the mathematical principles of test theory, and therefore are not as subjective (and therefore vulnerable to criticism) as previously discussed methods in increasing minority representation. However, for a variety of reasons, which I we will discuss, these methods have been difficult to implement.

The first option is called "within-group norming" (Doverspike et al., 2000; Hartigan & Wigdor, 1989; Sackett, 1996b; Sackett & Wilk, 1994; Sackett & Roth, 1991). Norming refers to a psychometric procedure that is used when developing psychological testing to determine the normal scores and distributions of a particular instrument. Let me give you an example. We know that a score of 100 is an average score and a score of 135 is a very high score if we are referring to an IQ test. But how do we know that? Because the test has been given to a sample of thousands of randomly selected individuals, and we have found out that the average, or mean score, of people who take the test is 100,* and only about 2 percent of the population score 135 or above. The process used to determine that information is called "norming" precisely because through it we can find out what the "norm" of the test is. In the case of intelligence tests, the norm is determined, the scoring of the test is adjusted to ensure that the mean score is always 100.

However, let us say that we want to take a successful IQ test in the United States, and export it, for instance, to England. In psychology, we know that we cannot just bring the test and use it. We have to norm the test again for the new population, because even though we know the normal score for the average person in the United States is 100, we cannot be certain this will be the case in England. Because of cultural and language differences, the English norm might be slightly different (higher or lower) than the American norm, and therefore the test would need to be re-normed for the new group. That is why, even with widely used and researched tests like the Weschler Intelligence Scales, psychologists in places like England or Canada (see, for example, Hunter, Yule, Urbanowicz, & Lansdown, 1989; Pugh & Boer, 1991) take the time to norm and validate the tests for their specific countries. Furthermore, intelligence and

---

*Even though the mean IQ of the population has increased over the past century, the test mean continues to be 100 because it is routinely adjusted for that purpose, since IQ tests are what we call "norm referenced tests." For more information, see, for example, Anastasi and Urbina, 1997.

personality tests routinely have different norming tables for different populations, usually based on race and gender.

Proponents of within-group norming (Hartigan & Wigdor, 1989; Sackett, 1996b; Sackett & Roth, 1991; Sackett & Wilk, 1994) argue that having different norms in selection tests (such as the SAT) for women and minorities is not only an accepted and sound psychometric practice, but would solve the performance gap issue once and for all. Unfortunately, language in the Civil Rights Act of 1991 seems to prohibit this practice and therefore it is no longer considered a viable alternative (Sackett, 1996a).

Another psychometric alternative to increase minority representation is called "banding" (Cascio, Outtz, & Zedeck, 1995; Igou, 2001; Sackett & Roth, 1991; Schmidt & Hunter, 1995; Zedeck, Cascio & Goldstein, 1996). In classical psychometric theory, it is assumed that no test is perfect, and therefore, any score a person receives is comprised both of a "true" score (what the real measure of the person's characteristic should be) and an "error" score (all other factors, including test error, that make the test score deviate from the true score). Because of this, scores that are relatively close to each other should not be compared. Mathematically, each error score is similar to the numbers you see in political polls, that have a "margin of error." Even though candidate A is 2 points ahead of candidate B, you will see the political commentators referring to a "statistical dead heat" or "too close to call." Test publishers will usually warn you of such margin of error. Test users will routinely ignore such a warning.

Proponents of banding to increase minority representation (Cascio et al., 1995; Zedeck et al., 1996) believe that because of such errors, instead of specific test scores, for instance, on the SAT, scores should be banded in broad groups. Just like final grades are calculated (that is, if you have 90 to 100 points you have an A, 80 to 89 a B, and so on), they argue that if you get, let us say, 1,300 to 1,600, you should be on band A, 1,000 to 1,299 on band B, and so on, therefore reducing the need to compare close scores. Research has found, however, that banding grades in this manner does not help increase minority representation in any significant way (Igou, 2001; Sackett & Roth, 1991) and therefore, proponents of banding suggest that within each band candidates could be selected using affirmative action criteria. Although this procedure has been found to significantly increase minority representation (Igou, 2001), the fact that it is not merely based on psychometric principles but also on the use of ethnic and gender factors makes it just as vulnerable as other nonpsychometric methods to criticism by opponents of affirmative action.

A Matter of Class?

Finally, one last idea that is being discussed is replacing ethnicity- and gender-based affirmative action with what is called "class-based" affirmative action (Kahlenberg, 1997; Kane, 1998). It has been argued for a long time that one of the major factors affecting low performance of minorities in education in general and in high-stakes tests in particular was socioeconomic status (SES; see, for example, Kohn, 1999; Muller & Schiller, 2000; Valencia & Suzuki, 2001). Since low SES has been found to be a strong mediating factor in the performance of minorities in testing, proponents of class-based affirmative action argue that we could still benefit minorities, yet avoid issues related to the legality of affirmative action by giving an advantage to the disadvantaged (Kahlenberg, 1997). However, critics of this approach argue that because attendance at the more selective colleges is in any event associated with higher SES and higher earnings, both for Whites and minorities, the policy would be ineffective. Kane (1998), in a statistical analysis of available data, contends that a switch to class-based affirmative action would not allow selective colleges to be able to maintain ethnic diversity, while Schrag (1997) reported that in states like California, class-based affirmative action would only attract more poor Asians students, who typically do much better in high-stakes testing, to replace the middle-class African Americans and Latinos.

Conclusion

The history and present course of affirmative action is confusing, plagued by ambiguity, and hijacked by political interests. From the beginning, affirmative action was purposefully unclear, and to this date, the lack of clarity has created chaos and contradiction in our political and legal systems. For example, Kahlenberg (1997) argues that the original purpose of affirmative action shifted during the 1970s, away from its original purpose of being a temporary system of ethnic preferences that was supposed to lead to a color-blind society. However, it is a lot less clear what the result of this shift was. With the multiple, changing definitions of affirmative action and the lack of a concise, clear language that would allow us to really assess its weaknesses and strengths, the American people have, to this date, very little unbiased, objective information to make informed decisions regarding the future of affirmative action. And lack of information can only lead to an increase in myths, misconceptions, and stereotypes.

Chapter 2

Affirmative Action: Myths and Misconceptions Revisited

There have been a number of papers written in the past few years regarding myths and misconceptions of affirmative action (see, for example, Jackson, 1995; Liu, 2002; Plous, 1996; Robinson, Seydel, & Douglas, 1998). Even though each one has focused on a different number of myths, a review of these papers presents essentially five big myths regarding affirmative action.

Myth 1: Affirmative Action Is Reverse Discrimination

One of the most important arguments of the antiaffirmative action camp is that affirmative action is, in effect, a form of "reverse discrimination." In other words, it is a zero-sum game: To give preference to some groups, you necessarily have to discriminate against others. However, this statement seems to apply to affirmative action only to the extent that affirmative action is considered a "hard" preference system of quotas. As I discussed in Chapter 1, hard affirmative action programs are, in fact, illegal and, for the most part, have not been proven to be any more effective than "soft" ones. So, what about soft programs? Can they also be a form of reverse discrimination?

To answer this question, we have to understand first what the term *reverse discrimination* actually means. Let us then begin by defining the word *discrimination*. One of the better-known definitions of this term in psychology was coined by Gordon Allport (1954). Allport explains that "discrimination includes any conduct based on a distinction made on grounds of natural or social categories, which have no relation either to individual capacities or merits, or the concrete behavior of the individual person" (p. 51). Furthermore, Grauman and Wintermantel (1989) elaborate by explaining that although the term discrimination in psychology can have a negative or a positive connotation, the major focus of the research in social psychology has been on how discrimination is used to deny access to some people, based on real or imaginary group membership, to outcome or resources granted to others. At least in this sense, therefore, the term reverse discrimination is an oxymoron.

The opponents of affirmative action, however, do not define reverse discrimination in quite the same way as it is defined in relation to psychology and other social sciences. (It is clear that the social scientific definition of discrimination would be useless in understanding the term.) For them, the term refers to "white males [being] denied jobs, rejected for promotion, or prevented from attending the college or professional school of their choice because slots were reserved for African Americans (or other minorities or women)" (Puddington, 1996). In other words, what the term reverse discrimination actually means is discrimination against White males. Therefore, by the definition of its opponents, affirmative action would be considered reverse discrimination because White males are being systematically denied admissions, hiring, and contracting. Therefore, it is necessary to look at the data to see if this assertion is correct.

There is no question that to this date minorities and women are still underrepresented in the top echelons of society. According to Jackson (1995), in 1995, 92 percent of Forbes 400 chief executive officers, 97 percent of school superintendents, 80 percent of tenured professors, and 99.9 percent of athletic team owners were White males. We would be hard-pressed to see a pattern of systematic discrimination against Whites in these "top-of-the-crop" occupations. However, opponents of affirmative action could argue that it is not at this level where the reverse discrimination is necessarily occurring. We have to look at the average American worker to understand how White male workers loose jobs due to affirmative action.

According to Plous (1996) not only is there no evidence of systematic loss of jobs among Whites, but in 1994, government data showed that there were less than 2 million unemployed African Americans in the United States, while there were over 100 million employed Whites. Plous further argues that "even if every unemployed African American worker were to displace a White worker, less than 2 percent of Whites would be affected" (p. 28).

Similarly, there is no evidence of systematic discrimination against Whites in higher education admissions. In a comprehensive analysis of higher education enrollment, Wilson (1998) compares the data for Whites and minorities. For example, for four-year colleges, she found that between 1976 and 1994, overall enrollment increased 23.5 percent. However, for the same period, enrollment of Whites increased by only 9.7 percent (not counting international students), while enrollment for African Americans increased 38.3 percent and for Latinos an astonishing 167.6 percent. Is that evidence of discrimination against Whites? According the Bureau of the Census, between the 1980 Census (data are not available for single years before 1980) and the 1994 population estimates, the White population of the United States increased about 11 percent, from about 194 million to 216 million, while the African American population increased 23 percent from about 26 million to 32 million, and the Hispanic population increased 85 percent from 14 to 26 million. These numbers do not show a disproportionate percentage "loss" in enrollment for White students (although they show a remarkable increase in minority enrollment, a point I will return to later). Furthermore, Wilson acknowledges there has been a relative decline of White representation in enrollment. However, his analysis shows that this decline is not due to affirmative action, but mainly to a massive increase in the numbers of Asian and international enrollments, which went from about 294,000 students in 1976 to 827,000 students in 1994.

This point is illustrated by Liu (2002). He makes an analysis regarding the odds of a White applicant being accepted into a top, highly competitive program. As an example, he uses the case that led to the *Regents of the Univ. of Cal. v. Bakke*. He points out that for Allan Bakke the probability of being rejected by the highly selective University of California–Davis's (UC–Davis) Medical School was about 97.3 percent with the affirmative action program as it stood. If UC–Davis had eliminated the program, as Bakke's supporters requested, his chances would have improved to only a 96.8 percent probability of being rejected. An insignificant difference. Moreover, since available spaces for college enrollment have actually increased in the decades since affirmative action has been implemented, it could be deducted that the probability of acceptance for a White applicant with or without affirmative action would remain practically unchanged. On the other hand, the dramatic results illustrated by the abrupt end of affirmative action programs in California and Texas indicate what the consequences would be for minorities.

In summary, even though one of the main arguments of the detractors of affirmative action is that it will lead to systematic discrimination of Whites and or White males, other than individual anecdotes, there is no supporting evidence to that claim.

Myth 2: Affirmative Action Has Failed in Increasing Female and Minority Representation

There is no question that there is still a gap between White males and women and minorities. For example, according to the Bureau of the Census (2002) in 2000, the median weekly earnings (MWE) for a male in the United States was $646, while the MWE for a female was $491, a ratio of 76 cents per woman for every dollar per man. Whites had an MWE in 2000 of $591, compared to an MWE of $468 for African Americans and an MWE of $396 for Hispanics (79 cents and 67 cents on the dollar, respectively).

The gap is also clearly evident if we look at occupational patterns. According to the Bureau of the Census (2002), females make up 46.5 percent of the workforce, while African Americans and Hispanics make up 11.3 percent and 10.7 percent, respectively. However, Table 2.1 illustrates how in several select fields there are still large disparities. However, the same data show the corresponding percentages of women and minorities working on these fields back in 1983.

Although Table 2.1 shows that there is indeed a disparity between the relative percentual representation of women and minorities in the workforce and in select fields, it also shows that there has been clear, and in some cases even spectacular, gains in the past two decades. To better understand these gains, we need to look at the math a little bit closer. If we calculate a ratio where we divide the relative percentual representation of a group in a specific field, by their relative percentual representation in the total workforce, parity (when both percents are

Table 2.1
Percent of Total People Working by Occupation, Gender, and Race

Field	Women 1983	Women 2000	African Americans 1983	African Americans 2000	Hispanics 1983	Hispanics 2000
Total	43.7	46.5	9.3	11.3	5.3	10.7
Executive, Administrative, and Managerial	32.4	45.3	4.7	7.6	2.6	5.4
All Professional Specialties	48.1	53.9	6.4	8.7	2.5	4.6
Physicians	15.8	27.9	3.2	6.3	4.5	3.7
Lawyers	15.3	29.6	2.6	5.4	0.9	3.9

equal) would equal 1. Numbers greater than one indicate overrepresentation, while numbers smaller than one, underrepresentation. For example, in 1983, omen represented 32.4 percent of executives, while they had a 43.7 percent representation in the total workforce. Their ratio would be 32.4/43.7 + .74. Therefore, the ratio for women in executive positions increased from .74 in 1983 to .97 in 2000, almost parity. Other impressive gains were made by women in law (from .35 to .63) and medicine (.36 to .60), and by African Americans in almost every field. The group with the least gains were Hispanics, whose ratio remained pretty much constant or slightly declined in almost every field except law, where it increased from .16 to .36.

Another statistic that illustrates the closing gap between Whites and minorities is the number of people below the poverty line. According to the Bureau of the Census (1999), in 1989, 8.3 percent of all White, non-Hispanics, 30.8 percent of African Americans, and 26.3 percent of Hispanics in the United States were below the poverty line. By 1998, the numbers had decreased slightly for Whites and Hispanics to 8.2 percent and 25.6 percent, respectively, and significantly for African Americans to 26.1 percent.

Social science research has also supported the effectiveness of affirmative action in increasing minority participation and removing discrimination barriers. For example, Murrell and Jones (1996), in a comprehensive assessment of the literature, concluded that affirmative action has been successful in diminishing some of the effects of prejudice, although they claim that the ultimate objective of affirmative action of achieving equality has not been reached. Also Pratkanis and Turner (1996) reviewed evidence that affirmative action had been "moderately" effective in increasing representation of minorities, although they propose a social psychological model to make it more successful. Similarly, Holzer and Neumark (1997), in an extensive study of companies in major metropolitan areas, concluded not only that affirmative action had a clear benefit in promoting and hiring women and minorities, but that this benefit came at no cost in productivity or efficiency for the companies. Finally, Plous (1996) cited reports from the USDOL and the Office of Federal Contract Compliance Programs supporting the effectiveness of affirmative action programs in increasing the representation of minorities and women in employment and federal contracting.

In summary, even though it is difficult to positively conclude that there is a causal relationship between affirmative action programs and the improvement of women and minorities in employment, education, and overall socioeconomic status, it is undeniable that since the inception of affirmative action, women and minorities have been able to attain a position that had eluded them for decades, if not centuries, before affirmative action was implemented.

Myth 3: Affirmative Action Actually Hurts Women and Racial Minorities

This particular misconception consists of two different arguments. The first is extrinsic to the beneficiaries, claiming that affirmative action affects minorities and women because, as a result of the preferential treatment they receive, other groups resent them and that increases prejudice. The second is intrinsic to the beneficiaries of affirmative action. The argument is that, since they are recipients of preferences, the awareness that they are held to a lower standard not only affects their self-esteem and self-conception, but also does not motivate them to excel since they know they can underperform and still be competitive. This myth also seems to be widespread. In fact, survey results (Witt, 1990) reveal that, in 1990, about 21 percent of White males believed affirmative action maintains the idea of minority inferiority, and 17 percent believed that it negatively affects minority's sense of accomplishment.

Although I will review the literature in this area more extensively in subsequent chapters, I will look at some of the general findings related to this particular myth. Doverspike and his colleagues (2000), in a review of the literature on the effects of affirmative action on the attributions of nonbeneficiaries, concluded that in fact some of the earlier psychological research supported the idea that non beneficiaries might have a lower opinion of people who were hired or admitted into a program because of affirmative action. However, this early research also found that the negative attributions were more likely to occur if the affirmative action program is defined as a hard preferential treatment program and if no information is provided about the individual qualifications of the beneficiary. Doverspike and colleagues (2000), however, noted that this research was done in experimental settings, in which participants "role-played" affirmative action situations, and were therefore devoid of the complexities of real affirmative action cases. Moreover, more recent, field-based research has found that there is almost no negative effect on the attitudes of nonbeneficiaries in real settings. Furthermore, these negative attitudes are even less likely to occur if information about the qualifications and performance of the beneficiary is emphasized, and if weaker types of affirmative action programs are used.

Similarly, Kravitz and her colleagues (1996) in a very comprehensive review of affirmative action research, also conclude that in experimental settings, nonbeneficiaries "typically view women and minorities selected through AAP to be less competent" (p. 36). However, they report that research suggests that this effect disappears by providing evidence of the beneficiaries' competence.

Regarding the second argument, that beneficiaries of affirmative action might experience lower self-esteem and feelings of self-efficacy due to their awareness of preferential treatment, early studies (see, for example, Chacko, 1982; Heilman, Simon & Repper, 1987; Nacoste & Arbor, 1985; Nacoste & Lehman, 1987) seemed to support this claim. However, just as before, most of these were laboratory studies in which participants were asked to role-play situations. A national field study by Taylor (1994) found, in fact, that the perceptions of

African American and White men and women did not differ significantly when it came to self-assessment or self-esteem. In fact, the literature review by Kravitz et al. (1996) concluded that "programs that
provide explicit, unambiguous, and focused evidence of recipient
qualifications . . . do not appear to impair task choice or self-evaluations of performance and ability" (p. 45). Doverspike et al. (2000), in
turn, concluded that even though some research suggested that there
were some costs for the beneficiaries of affirmative action, these
"costs are primarily psychological and may be relatively short in du-
ration" (p. 138). Finally, Plous (1996) argued that affirmative action
"may actually *raise* the self-esteem of women and minorities by providing them with employment and opportunities for advancement"
(p. 29). In conclusion, not only is there no clear evidence that there
actually are any deleterious effects for women and minorities of being
the beneficiaries of affirmative action, but even if we acknowledge
the possibility that there are, they are clearly outweighed by the positive effects that affirmative action overall can have in the lives of its
beneficiaries.

Myth 4: Affirmative Action Is No Longer Necessary

This myth directly contradicts Myth 2. Basically, the principle is that
whatever debt the American society had with minorities and women
for past discrimination is more than paid. Questions such as "How
long should we keep paying for slavery?" are common examples.

This myth assumes that the gates of opportunity for minorities
and women are finally fully open; that prejudice, discrimination, and
racism no longer exist; and that affirmative action is only some sort
of "compensation" for past, no longer existent, wrongdoing. Furthermore, while proponents of this particular misconception acknowledge that a social, economical, and educational gap still exists,
they explain this gap in terms of factors other than prejudice and/or
discrimination, and therefore outside of the spirit of affirmative action. These explanations carry the assumption that lower performance is "person centered" and linked to ethnic minority or gender
membership, while external factors limiting minorities' development
are held largely blameless, a framework known as "deficit thinking"
(Valencia, 1997). They range from those who emphasize ethnic-cul-

tural explanations (Alexander, Entwisle, & Bedinger, 1994; Artiles & Trent, 1994; Ogbu, 2002) to those who stress cognitive (Kramer, Allen, & Gergen, 1995; Nelson-Le Gall & Jones, 1990) or even biological (Beckum, 1983; Herrnstein & Murray, 1994) factors.

Most of the views regarding genetics and ethnic culture as the culprits of the underperformance of minorities have since been strongly challenged or outright refuted (see, for example, Cohen, 1998; Devlin, Fienberg, & Resnick, 2002; Fish, 2002; Horn, 2002; Neisser, 1998; Reifman, 2000), and persuasive arguments have been made to explain the performance gap in terms of factors such as test bias (see, for example, Suzuki & Valencia, 1997; Valencia & Salinas, 2000), socioeconomic status and educational opportunity (Stricker, Rock, Pollack, & Wenglinsky, 2002), mainstream American culture, as opposed to ethnic culture (Cohen, 1998), and psychological factors such as stereotype threat (J. Aronson, 2002; Steele & Aronson, 1995). But regardless of the specific cause or combination of causes that lead to the underperformance of ethnic minorities and women, as long as we recognize that it is the result of social structures, attitudes, and stereotypes in America and not of deficits in the underrepresented groups, we have the obligation of correcting for those inequalities. And as I have discussed previously, affirmative action is mostly an attempt at this correction, and only vaguely a form of "compensation."

Today, it is clear that only through affirmative action can we achieve the diversity we need to adequately serve the American public in critical areas such as education, law, and medicine. As the recent experiences with education in Texas and in California show, eliminating affirmative action will turn back the clock to a time when underrepresented minorities and women were also underserved, ignored, and discriminated against because they had no access to the social and political institutions that shape our society. For example, according to Cornwell (1998), after the elimination of affirmative action in the University of California System, "the number of minority students offered places at California's top public universities has plummeted by more than half" (p. 8). Cornwell explains that, for example, in the flagship UC–Berkeley, the number of admission offers to African American students fell to 191 in 1998, compared to 562 in 1997, before the elimination of affirmative action. Even more dramatically, the number of offers to Latino/a applicants dropped from 1,266 in 1997 to only 60 in 1998. I have reviewed similar numbers for Texas and other California schools in this book. It is clear that eliminating affirmative action at this stage would result in a significant decrease in the number of minorities who can access positions of service (such as teaching, medicine, or law) or influence (such as politics) that over time will have a cumulative effect on the quality of life of underrepresented groups. Although we could argue about the means by which we should realize it, it is clear that the ultimate goal of affirmative action, equality, and equal opportunity for all in America has not been achieved yet, and until it is, or until a viable alternative to it is found, affirmative action is very much necessary.

Myth 5: Affirmative Action Is Not Supported by a Majority of the People

At the beginning of this book, I referred to a poll that was conducted in Connecticut regarding affirmative action. This poll was conducted by the Center for Survey Research and Analysis (2000) of the University of Connecticut, but was in fact funded and designed by the Connecticut Association of Scholars, a local chapter of the National Association of Scholars, a conservative group that opposes affirmative action.

The questions were asked to over one thousand faculty from state universities in Connecticut, and were worded in a way similar to California's Proposition 209. The interviewers asked whether the interviewee supported the granting of preferences based on race, ethnicity, or gender, either in the hiring of faculty or in student admissions.

The results were very sobering, and provided quite a bit of political ammunition to the detractors of affirmative action. Depending on the type of university, between 52 percent and 75 percent of faculty "opposed" granting preference in faculty hiring based on race, sex, or ethnicity, while 47 percent to 73 percent opposed it in student admissions. The results of this poll were represented as clear evidence that faculty opposed affirmative action, and dozens of other polls conducted in a similar manner clearly supported the myth that affirmative action is no longer supported by the majority of the American people. Or is it?

In 1995, the Feminist Majority Foundation (Harris, 1995), set up to test this proposition as the drive to end affirmative action in California, was gaining momentum. They began their extensive study of over thirteen hundred adults in the United States and eight hundred more adults in California by asking if participants supported language identical to that of California's Proposition 209:

The state will not use race, sex, color, ethnicity, or national origin as a criterion for either discriminating against, or granting preferential treatment to, any individual or group in the operation of the State's system of public employment, public education, or public contracting." (cited in Harris, 1995, p. 3)

Sure enough, the study found that by an overwhelming majority the American people supported the language of the proposition by 81 percent to 11 percent. At first glance, this seems to support the conception that the American people do not support affirmative action anymore. But if we look at these findings in more depth, they paint a very different picture. The study asked three more questions of the participants:

1. Would you still favor this proposition if it would outlaw all affirmative action programs for women and minorities?
2. Would you still favor this proposition if it would discourage or even end programs to help women and minorities to achieve equal opportunities in education and employment?
3. Would you still favor this proposition if it would discourage or even end programs to give women and minority-owned businesses a chance to compete with other businesses on getting government contracts? (Harris, 1995, p. 3)

The results of the study are quite dramatic. In the first case, support for the initiative collapses to 29 percent while opposition rises to 58 percent. In the second and third cases, support declines to only 31 percent and opposition increases to 56 percent.

Similarly, Steeh and Krysan (1996), in a comprehensive review of the survey data from 1970 to 1995, concluded that the level of support for affirmative action programs tended to fluctuate widely depending on the way the survey question was framed. Questions framed in terms of preferences or quotas received relatively low support, usually around

20 percent to 30 percent, while questions framed in terms of educational assistance, job training, and outreach yielded support in the upper 60 percent to lower 80 percent range.

Plous (1996) makes another important distinction between support to *eliminate* affirmative action and support to *reform* affirmative action. In a review of several surveys conducted in 1995, Plous found that when the American public is given the choice to "mend" or "reform" affirmative action, support for reform hovers in different polls from the high 50s to the high 60s. On the other hand, support for eliminating or ending all affirmative action remains at the mid to upper 20s.

Finally, more current polls also suggest that support for affirmative action has remained stable since 1995. A review of CNN/Gallup/ *USA Today* polls from 1995 to 2000 (see Table 2.2) indicate that when asked "Do you generally favor or oppose affirmative action programs for women and minorities?" those in favor remained constant at around 55 percent to 58 percent.

Once again, it looks as if the misconception that Americans do not support affirmative action develops from a problem of definition. When Americans are asked about their support regarding "preferential treatment" or affirmative action is defined in terms of "quotas" (hard preference affirmative action, which in any case is prohibited by law), it appears that there is a majority who oppose it. However, if affirmative action is defined in terms of support, removal of barriers, or even if the question is simply asked "Do you favor or oppose affirmative action?" then a clear majority of Americans support it.

Table 2.2
CNN/Gallup/*USA Today* Poll (Latest: January 13–16, 2000)

Date	Favor	Oppose	No Opinion
January 2000	58 percent	33 percent	9 percent
November 1997	56 percent	36 percent	8 percent
March 1995	55 percent	34 percent	11 percent

Note: N = 1,027 adults nationwide. MoE ± 3.

Conclusion

As can be seen, the confusion regarding the definition of affirmative action is compounded by a series of myths and misconceptions. These misconceptions sometimes emerge from a lack of knowledge by the American public, not only of affirmative action, but of the effects that it has for the beneficiaries, the nonbeneficiaries, and society as a whole. But sometimes those misconceptions stem from a deliberate attempt by political groups and individuals with political agendas to manipulate the debate in a certain direction. This premeditated attempt at influencing public opinion by the use of misconstrued beliefs regarding the attributes of groups of people (for example, minorities or women) or the characteristics of social programs (for example, affirmative action, equal opportunity) is what we refer to as "the politics of stereotype."

Chapter 3

Affirmative Action and Psychology

As I discussed in Chapter 2, there is ample evidence that affirmative action has been, so far, fairly successful in increasing the representation of minorities. It has been especially meaningful because it has allowed women and minorities to reach positions in which they can serve as role models for younger generations, and in which they can significantly affect the decision-making process that will lead to future policies and social practices in reducing discrimination and increasing equality in America.

However, even some of its supporters agree that affirmative action was meant to be only a temporary remedy with the ultimate goal of ending inequality. For example, Patterson (1998) believes that although affirmative action provides minorities with "otherwise unavailable access to critical social networks and entry-level openings" (p. 43), it is only a middle-term solution to the problems of social, residential and cultural integration of minorities, and that "the program is supposed to be self-canceling: its success should obviate the need for it" (p. 45). He advocates setting clear goals and a time limit on affirmative action in order to make it more fair and effective. Similarly, Rhode (1997) sees affirmative action as a "crucial element in promoting diversity among policy leaders" (p. 12). However, she believes that it should not and could not be the primary solution for the inequalities of minorities and women. She suggests that we should search for ways to decrease the need for affirmative action, and that

greater efforts should be placed in addressing the root social and economic causes of underrepresentation.

As a social scientist, I believe, therefore, that to better advocate
for the rights of underrepresented groups, we have to objectively look
at affirmative action. Affirmative action is clearly needed, and currently, it is the best alternative we have to end inequalities in America.
However, only if we recognize that, as any other remedy, affirmative
action has the potential of having "side effects" and unintended consequences, will we be able to achieve its ultimate goal of social equality. Therefore, this chapter presents an account, from a psychological
point of view, of the empirical evidence examining both the intended
and the unintended consequences of affirmative action.

Has Affirmative Action Helped Decrease Negative Attitudes and Stereotypes of Minorities?

To answer this question, we must first understand what the psychological processes are that lead to a decrease in stereotypes and prejudice. Perhaps the first attempt to look at prejudice reduction from a
psychological perspective was suggested by the renowned psychologist
Gordon Allport (1954), when he proposed the "contact hypothesis."
Allport believed that prejudice could be reduced by simply increasing
the contact between the prejudiced and the target groups. Years later,
a more elaborate model based on the contact hypothesis was developed by Zajonc (1968). The "mere exposure effect" could help us better understand how affirmative action can lead to a reduction in
stereotypes. According to this model, people have a tendency to like
any particular stimulus more after they have been repeatedly exposed
to it. For example, in some experiments, the more times participants
were exposed to a stranger, the more they liked him, even though there
was no other interaction between the subject and the stranger
(Saegert, Swap, & Zajonc, 1973). Hamm and his colleagues (Hamm,
Baum, & Nikels, 1975) attempted to test if the mere exposure effect
specifically improved attitudes across racial lines. They presented pho-
tographs of African American and White subjects to undergraduate
students, and found that regardless of the race of the subject in the
photograph, repeated exposure enhanced the interpersonal attitude of
the participant toward the subject in the picture. More recently, Born-

stein (1993), in a review of the literature, concluded that exposure to members of a prejudiced group (or "out-group") is enough to increase people's attitudes toward that out-group.

Another theory that supports a possible connection between affirmative action and stereotype reduction is called the "disconfirmation" theory (Stephan, 1985), which is built on the concept that people naturally tend to downplay the differences which exist between the people in the group we belong to, or in-group, a cognitive process known as "assimilation." We either ignore these differences, or de-emphasize them. On the other hand, people tend to emphasize the differences between the in-group and the out-groups, a process known as "contrast." Stereotypes and prejudice emerge from a cycle of assimilation and contrast as we see ourselves more and more similar to the people in our in-group and increasingly different from the people in the out-group (a process that could eventually lead to dehumanizing the out-group altogether). In a nutshell, disconfirmation is an intervention strategy that consists of providing information to the person who *disproves* these differences. The implication is that by providing evidence that shows that the out-group is not actually as different from you as you believe, you might reevaluate your beliefs and begin to reduce the stereotypes.

Weber and Crocker (1983) investigated three types of disconfirmation models for their effectiveness-reducing stereotypes. In the bookkeeping model, stereotype-relevant information is used to alter the stereotype gradually; in the conversion model, stereotypes change dramatically as a result of situations that radically challenge the stereotype; and finally, in the subtyping model, new cognitive structures are developed to "accommodate" information that contradicts the stereotype, avoiding dissonance with the existing stereotype. Weber and Crocker found that when evidence inconsistent with the stereotype is presented in a concentrated manner, subtyping is likely to occur, leaving the original stereotype unchallenged. On the other hand, if evidence is presented in a disperse manner (as would be the case in contact resulting from affirmative action), bookkeeping is more likely to happen, slowly changing the stereotype.

One final area of research that would suggest that affirmative action should help reduce ethnic and gender stereotypes is the research focused on the effect of behavior on attitudes. According to this research, our actions, even if they are involuntary or just feigned or simulated, are a powerful factor in affecting our attitudes. For example, some researchers have found that if we role-play a certain part, we tend to modify our beliefs to match those of the role. The best-known example of this phenomenon is the famous experiment by Phillip Zimbardo (Haney, Banks, & Zimbardo, 1973) in which a number of college students volunteered to simulate a prison environment. They were randomly divided into guards and prisoners. However, after a couple of days in which the volunteers played their roles, they began to exhibit behaviors that were consistent with a "real" situation (the guards abused and mistreated the prisoners, the prisoners became submissive or broke down). The behaviors became so outrageous that Zimbardo was compelled to halt the study after only six days. The students later reported actually developing strong negative feelings and contempt for their simulated jailers and prisoners, respectively. Apparently, people have an internal need to reconcile both the behavior and the attitude, and since it would be hard to justify a particular behavior when we do not believe in it, being forced to act in a positive (or negative) way will, in turn, shape our attitude to reduce conflict, a process known as "cognitive dissonance." In any event, rsearch on this area suggests that if we display positive behaviors toward the out-group, even if these behaviors are forced on us by policy or law, it could have some positive effects in our attitudes as well.

Specific research in the area of stereotype and prejudice reduction has mostly supported these theoretical models. Tal-Or, Boninger, and Gleicher (2002) completed a comprehensive review of the literature related to prejudice reduction after intergroup contact. They provide numerous examples of instances in which prejudice is reduced through intergroup participation, and analyze a successful model used in a contact program to reduce prejudice between Arabs and Israelis. In addition, Fiske (2000), in a review of several studies, argues that prejudice and stereotypes can be reduced through *individual-level interdependence*, which refers to having contact in a context in which participants from opposing groups have to cooperate, like participating in the same team. Fiske believes that this individual-level interdependence, as opposed to the mere contact or group-level interaction, forces the individual to pay attention to the individual attributes of the other person, which in turn reduces the dependence on stereotypical thoughts and therefore results in a more complex evaluation of the other group. On the other hand, she also suggests that group-level interdependence, which refers to groups competing against each other (she uses the example of a sports team), does not help reduce stereotypical thinking and prejudice because it does not force the individual to evaluate the persons from the out-group on an individual basis.

Finally, although there is very little research regarding the specific effects of affirmative action on ethnic and gender stereotypes, a small number of studies strongly suggest that the repeated, systematic and interdependent contact between minority and majority groups has had a positive effect in reducing stereotypes and prejudice. For example, to investigate the relationship between prejudicial beliefs and attitudes toward affirmative action, Belliveau (1996) reviewed several studies from the early 1990s related to the attitudes of people working in companies affected by affirmative action. She discovered that when companies had strong affirmative action policies and in which the individual contact between beneficiaries and nonbeneficiaries is the greatest, instead of opposition to affirmative action, employees in fact had a significantly greater level of endorsement of affirmative action. These conclusions are also supported in a study by Parker, Christiansen, and Baltes (1997), in which they surveyed over six thousand federal employees. Because of the nature of the federal government, these workers must have significant individual-level interdependence with individuals from different groups and ethnicities, and sure enough, Parker and his colleagues found that among White men, affirmative action was not associated with either a loss in career and promotion opportunities or negative attitudes toward work. Furthermore, for ethnic minorities and women, support for affirmative action was positively related to positive attitudes and perceptions of increased career opportunities.

Dovidio and Gaertner (1996) also review the literature in an attempt to determine if affirmative action is still needed considering the change from the more overt, traditional racial prejudices to the more subtle contemporary racial attitudes (see Chapter 4). Dovidio and Gaertner conclude that even though the nature of contemporary prejudices is less obvious and deliberate than in the past, it still can produce obstacles to the advancement and development of ethnic minorities. Moreover, they suggest that because of the contact and individual-level interdependence they foster, affirmative action programs can actually help reduce contemporary biases effectively.

Has Affirmative Action Affected
the Performance of Minorities?

One of the arguments of critics of affirmative action is that when beneficiaries know that they are given "preference," their motivation to succeed, and consequently their performance, declines. On the other hand, supporters of affirmative action will argue that it actually increases performance, first, directly, by providing opportunities in education, training and development to beneficiaries, and, second, indirectly, by allowing minorities to ascend to positions in which they can serve as role models and motivate other groups of beneficiaries to excel. For example, Bill Nichols, of *USA Today*, (2001) refers to Colin Powell, who is a beneficiary of affirmative action, as a "national icon and a beacon of hope for many African-Americans" (p. 7A) because of the example of success that he represents. However, and regardless of the political rhetoric, is there any research that supports either claim? Does affirmative action actually have an effect on the performance of minorities?

Negative Effects

One of the first studies to research the effect of affirmative action on the performance of the beneficiaries was one conducted by Leonard (1984), in which he examined the effect that the increase of women and minority workers in manufacturing firms (due to affirmative action) would have on productivity. Although he did not review individual performance, he discovered that the increase in the number of affirmative action beneficiaries on a company did not have an effect on the efficiency or productivity of the firm. Another early study was performed by Steel and Lovrich (1987). In this study, they researched the efficiency of police departments and the effect that the increase in the number of women hired due to affirmative action had on the delivery of police services. Just like Leonard, Steel and Lovrich found that the increase in the number of women had no negative effect on the efficiency of police departments.

A more recent study regarding the effect of affirmative action on organizational performance was conducted by Silva and Jacobs (1993). They examined data from a number of companies, and found that hiring minority applicants at a rate equal to or slightly greater than their representation in the applicant pool did not result in a significant loss of performance. However, they also found that if minorities were hired in a proportion much larger than their relative representation in the applicant pool, the discrepancy between the performance of minorities and nonminorities tended to increase. This effect was probably due to the fact that in their desire to comply with affirmative action and equal employment guidelines, many companies hired a large number of only minimally qualified applicants just because of their minority status. Nevertheless, this study too focuses on overall organizational impact rather than effects on individual performance.

The first study to look specifically at the effects of affirmative action on individual performance was conducted by Nacoste and Arbor (1985). In this study, they investigated the effect of a selection process based on merit versus preference in female college students participating in a cognitive task. Male and female college students were told that they were selected to participate in a cognitive exercise either because they scored high on a previous test (merit) or because more participants of their gender were needed, even though their scores were not particularly high (preference). He found no significant differences in performance of the students, neither men nor women, who believed they were selected due to preference versus the ones selected by merit. Although this study sheds some light on the role of "preferential" selection on task performance, it was based on the general principle of preferential selection rather than the specific effects of affirmative action.

Research that specifically focuses on the effect of affirmative action on performance was reviewed by Turner and Pratkanis (1994). Although they conclude that the evidence on the impact of affirmative action on either individual or organizational performance is inconsistent, their review supports the thesis that when the qualifications of the beneficiary are made clear, explicit, and unambiguous, and the task is dependent on the capability of the individual, there are no negative effects on performance.

Heilman and Alcott (2001) conducted two studies regarding the effect of preferential selection on the performance of women on an academic task. About 150 female undergraduate students who were selected for an academic task, were told that a confederate of the study thought they were selected for the task because of preferential treatment and not qualifications. Heilman and Alcott found that this knowledge led the students to believe that the confederate had a negative expectation regarding their performance. They also found that if the female students were uncertain regarding their qualifications to complete the task, the belief of the confederate impaired their performance. However, when the opposite was true, and the students were confident of their ability to solve the task successfully, the knowledge that the confederate believed they were selected due to preference actually prompted better performance and an increase in motivation to make a good impression on the confederate. This study supports previous research suggesting that when preference is the only variable used for selection, it might prompt negative consequences. However, when the beneficiaries are confident of their abilities, preferential selection does not seem to have any negative effects and might even have a positive, effort-maximizing effect.

Two more studies that looked at preferential selection and academic performance were conducted by Brown, Charnsangavej, Keough, Newman, and Rentfrow (2000). In the first study, female students were recruited to be group leaders in a problem-solving task. They were divided into groups based on three conditions. In the first, they were told that they were selected just because of gender; in the second, because of gender and ability; and in the third, just by chance. Women in the first condition had a significant decline in performance when compared to participants in the two other conditions.

In the second study, Brown and his colleagues gave questionnaires to a multiethnic sample of undergraduate students, and looked at their GPA. They found that if the students believed they had benefited from affirmative action in their admission to college, there was a negative correlation with their GPA. However, this study did not directly look at the effect of affirmative action but just at the individual *belief* of having benefited from preferential admissions. Therefore, it is consistent with previous research that suggests that it is not affirmative action per se that affects performance, but both the social stereotype (through stereotype threat, discussed in Chapter 4) and the individual's belief of their abilities, as a member of a minority, that triggers the negative effects. This idea is supported by the data collected by Brown and his colleagues that showed a strong negative relationship between the suspicion of preferential treatment and academic self-confidence, and a positive relationship between self-confidence and GPA.

This link between the belief of minorities in their abilities and evaluation of performance is further reinforced in a study by Mayo and Christenfeld (1999). They conducted an experiment in which minority and nonminority college students were divided into two groups. Participants in the first group performed a reading comprehension task, while participants in the second group performed a creativity task. Mayo and Christenfeld found no actual difference in performance between the minority and the nonminority participants in either task. However, they found a number of interesting differences in the estimate of performance of the students from ethnic minorities. First, the individual believed they would do worse than other minority students regardless of the task. And second, they also estimated that their ethnic group would do worse than the nonminority participants.

Although the research I have discussed so far is inconclusive in many areas, it certainly fails to confirm any type of negative effect in performance due to affirmative action, either in productivity or in academic tasks. Furthermore, although in some cases the belief of preferential selection seems to have a detrimental effect when the beneficiary is actually confident of his or her abilities, this belief seems to have the opposite effect of motivating and perhaps improving performance. Is it actually possible, therefore, that affirmative action and other programs benefiting minorities can help improve performance rather than hinder it?

Improving Performance

Theoretically speaking, affirmative action could have a positive effect on performance either in a direct or an indirect manner. Directly, affirmative action and other programs intended to help minorities could, by granting access to minorities to selective programs and education, improve their qualifications and therefore their overall performance, both academically (especially in graduate and professional programs) and professionally. Indirectly, having more qualified minorities in positions in which they serve as role models, but more importantly, as service providers themselves, should have an overall positive effect on performance and achievement. Teachers, lawyers, or mental health professionals, for example, who are familiar with the culture and customs of minority groups, should be more effective and efficient at servicing these populations.

Interestingly, I was unable to find any experimental studies that actually looked at the direct connection between affirmative action and improved performance. The study by Taylor (1994), which looked at the 1990 General Social Survey data, found evidence of positive effects of affirmative action in occupational ambition, but it did not look directly at performance. There is also plenty of evidence of other indicators, such as income or socioeconomic status, improving due to affirmative action (see, for example, Pollard & O'Hare, 1999; Roberts, 1995), but still, no empirical evidence of a direct link between affirmative action and performance.

Some studies have looked at other programs that provide educational training and access to minorities and improvements in performance. For example, in a review of thirty-eight studies about the long-term effects of early-childhood programs for minority and low-income children, Barnett (1998), found that they had significant, long-lasting positive effects on achievement and academic success. He also concluded, using a cost-benefit analysis model, that the long-term economic benefits of these programs far exceeds their initial costs. At the undergraduate level, some research also has found that increased access and training can improve the performance of minorities in college admissions tests. For example, Fields (1997) reviews the results of the Equity 2000 Program, a program sponsored by the publishers of the SAT, the Educational Testing Service. Traditionally, minority children have had less access to higher level "advanced placement" and "honors" courses. Fields concluded that following this program, which provides minority children with the opportunity and encourages them to take higher level math courses, improved both their school achievement and their SAT scores.

One of the biggest dangers that detractors of affirmative action express is the possibility that admitting more "underqualified" minorities to professional programs, such as law or medicine, might later undermine the overall quality of services because it will produce less-qualified professionals. The research, however, fails to support that claim. Moreover, it once again points out the inadequacy of the instruments we use to judge "merit" in academic admissions. For example, Whitworth and Barrientos (1990) examined the undergraduate GPAs and the Graduate Record Examination (GRE) admission exam scores of Hispanic and White students who had been admitted to graduate programs. They did find, as expected, that the average GRE and GPA scores of the White students was higher than that of the Hispanic students. However, and more interesting, is that not only did they find that the GRE+GPA formula had very little validity to predict the graduate performance of all the students, it was even worse at predicting the performance of the Hispanics. Furthermore, they discovered that the GRE alone had no relationship at all with graduate performance, pointing out once again the uselessness of the exam as a predictive or even a merit criteria.

Kulatunga-Moruzi and Norman (2002) conducted a similar study but looked at a number of admission criteria to medical schools in Canada and then compared it to the students' performance in their licensing exams. The study found only moderate correlations between some individual sections of the Medical College Admission Test (MCAT) and sections of the licensing exam, but failed to support the use of MCAT as a solid predictor of performance. Basco, Gilbert, Chessman, and Blue (2000) also looked at medical students, and failed to find a predictive relationship among the MCAT, interview scores, or previous academic performance and the Objective Structure Clinical Examination, a third-year medical student comprehensive exam of clinical ability. Although these studies did not look specifically at the performance of minorities, they did question our overall use of admissions criteria that have too often been equated with merit but, in fact, have no validity as predictors of performance.

Kidder (2001) looked at a similar question for law students, and focused on their effect on minority students. He examined a sample of applicants to fifteen highly selective law schools to study whether the Law School Admissions Test (LSAT) is a valid predictor of law school performance for minorities, or if, in fact, it is ethnically biased. He concluded that the exam is biased since the performance gap between ethnic groups is larger than differences in any other measure, including undergraduate GPA, law school grades, or various other indicators of success in the legal profession. These results are also supported in a study by Wightman (1997). She examined the consequences of abandoning affirmative action on law school admissions by looking at applicants' data. Not only did she conclude that using admissions criteria the way they are used in most law schools today, relying heavily on

LSAT and GPA scores, would have a tremendously detrimental impact on admissions of minority students, but she also found that those criteria had, once again, no relationship with subsequent measures of success such as graduation rates or bar exam scores.

In summary, the research shows that there is very little evidence supporting the claim that affirmative action might have a significantly negative impact either in organizational performance, or in individual performance, achievement, or success of the beneficiaries.

Has Affirmative Action Increased the Negative Stereotype of the Beneficiaries?

In Chapter 2, I briefly discussed some of the misconceptions regarding the effects of affirmative action on the perceptions of the nonbeneficiaries. In this section I will take a more in-depth look at what psychological research can tell us regarding the increase in stereotypes and prejudice as a result of affirmative action.

One of the first studies to look at the question of the attitudes of nonbeneficiaries toward the beneficiaries of affirmative action was conducted by Jacobson and Koch in 1977. In this experimental study, male undergraduate students were assigned a female confederate to work with. The participants were divided into three groups. In the first group, the female confederates were "assigned" to become the leaders of the pair because of their gender, simulating an affirmative action preference (also known as an "assigned leader papradigm"). In the second group, the "assignment" was supposedly done randomly; and in the third group, the male participants were told the assignment was done on the basis of performance on a task the female had completed before the experiment. Jacobson and Koch's results suggested overall that perception of preference colored the opinion of the participants. For example, if the group leader was assigned using a supposed "preference" criterion, and failed in the task, her male partner would assign more blame. Conversely, if the female leader succeeded, her partner would grant less credit. In contrast, if the group leader was assigned using a "performance" criterion, the male partner would give more credit and assign less blame to their female leaders.

This tendency to have a more negative opinion of a beneficiary was supported in further research. For example, Summers (1991) studied whether the affirmative action policy of an organization could affect people's evaluations of the beneficiaries. Summers divided male and female undergraduate students into small groups, and then provided each group with information about an organization's affirmative action policies and about a woman in this organization who had been recently promoted. He discovered that both male and female participants tended to evaluate the woman's qualifications more negatively if the organization had a strong affirmative action policy.

Heilman and her colleagues (Heilman, Block, & Lucas, 1992) also examined whether affirmative action aggravated the negative stereotype of beneficiaries. In one experimental study, undergraduate students reviewed employment applications of male and female individuals who supposedly had been recently hired by a company. When the fictitious employee was female and described as being associated with an affirmative action program, it had a negative effect on the participants' evaluation of her qualifications when compared to identical qualifications of someone not associated with affirmative action. In a second investigation by Heilman and her associates, this one a field study, they interviewed White male workers about their opinions of colleagues. Heilman found that when the workers suspected the colleagues had been helped by affirmative action, it also affected negatively not only their job evaluations, but also their opinions regarding personal attributes and career outlook of the beneficiaries. Another experimental study by Heilman (Heilman, McCullough, & Gilbert, 1996), also with undergraduate students in an evaluation of simulated situations, further supported that preferential selection due to affirmative action by itself can have a negative effect on the evaluations of the beneficiaries.

A more recent study by Maio and Esses (1998) used an original approach to separate affirmative action as a concept from the attitudes of participants toward specific gender or ethnic groups. They gave undergraduate students positive information about a fabricated immigrant group. Half of the students were told the group could benefit from affirmative action, and the other half were told the group could not benefit. Maio and Esses found that the group that was told the immigrants would benefit from affirmative action tended to hold less favorable opinions of the immigrant group in particular and were even less supportive of immigration in general.

Gilbert and Stead (1999) questioned whether the opposition to affirmative action was a specific disagreement with the principle of diversity or if it was just opposition to the specific program. In two studies with undergraduate business students, they highlighted the difference between affirmative action, and *diversity management*, a model designed to ensure diversity in the workplace but that does not have all the negative connotations already ascribed to affirmative action. Gilbert and Stead found that even though diversity management still is based on the concept of increasing gender and ethnic representation, it did not have the same negative effects of affirmative action since women and minorities hired under diversity management received more positive evaluations than those employed under affirmative action.

Up to this point, there seems to be consistent evidence that affirmative action does have a negative effect on the perceptions and attitudes of the nonbeneficiaries. However, most of these studies have been done in experimental conditions that simplify the conditions, or look very specifically at affirmative action as a program with all its myths and misconceptions. What happens when we broaden the question or look at real-life situations in a more complex setting?

In a comprehensive review of the literature, Taylor-Carter, Doverspike, and Cook (1996) argued that if, on the one hand, there is convincing evidence that there are some negative perceptions on the part of the beneficiaries that can be potentially exacerbated by affirmative action, on the other hand, a number of simple intervention strategies at the organizational level can all but eliminate that effect. They specifically point to diversity training, team integration of beneficiaries and nonbeneficiaries, and clearly communicating information about the qualifications of the beneficiaries as strategies that have been supported in the literature as being successful in eliminating stigmas and negative stereotypes related to affirmative action.

These conclusions by Taylor-Carter and her colleagues were further supported by subsequent research. For example, Heilman, Battle, Keller, and Lee (1998) conducted three studies with undergraduate and graduate students. In these studies, participants were presented with information regarding different simulated evaluation situations (for example, in the first and third studies, the leader paradigm method, similar to the one used in Jacobson and Koch in 1977, was used, while in the second study, a selection model like the one used in Heilman et al., 1992, was used). In addition to the information regarding the selection (preference versus merit), some participants were also presented with information making clear that even if preference was used as a selection criteria, the qualifications of the selected individual were central in making the decision. Heilman found that if the qualification information was not included, many of the negative outcomes I have discussed occurred. However, when the qualifications information was added, it alleviated most of the negative effects of affirmative action.

Traver (1999) reports similar results in a study in which undergraduate students were presented with a fabricated paradigm in which a male or female police officer performed different job-related tasks. Some of the participants were told that the female police officer was hired through an affirmative action program, while others were just told the female police office was hired. Consistent with the results of previous studies, Traver found that when the only information given about the female police officer was that she was hired through affirmative action, male participants tended to rate the officer as less competent. However, when clear information regarding the qualifications of the officer was provided together with the affirmative action information, it eliminated the difference in the evaluation of the affirmative action–hired officer and the other officers.

In summary, even though there is consistent evidence that affirmative action can potentially have a negative effect on the perception of the beneficiaries by the nonbeneficiaries, it is also clear that with some very simple and practically costless strategies these effects can be mostly eliminated. Since most of the real-life affirmative action cases are of the barrier-elimination or the soft-preferential treatment types, in which ethnicity or gender are only used incidentally or as only one factor to differentiate among otherwise qualified applicants, it would be very simple to provide unambiguous information about the beneficiary's qualifications to offset any negative effects of affirmative action.

Does Affirmative Action Affect the Self-Esteem/Self-Concept of the Beneficiaries?

The other major criticism that opponents of affirmative action have expressed regarding the negative effects of affirmative action refers to the consequences of being a beneficiary of a preference program in the actual self-esteem and self-concept of the beneficiaries themselves. The logic is that, when an individual knows that he or she was hired or admitted to a program not because of their qualification but because of ethnic or gender preferences, that could damage his or her sense of accomplishment and self-worth.

One of the first studies to examine this question was conducted by Chacko (1982). In his study, he collected data from fifty-five female mangers in several companies, and discovered that if the women perceived that they were hired or promoted because of preferential treatment, their scores in a number of job satisfaction measures (such as satisfaction with their position and organizational commitment) were lower than the scores of women who perceived they were hired solely on the strength of their qualifications.

Another study that supports these findings was performed by Nacoste and Arbor (1985). In this study, female undergraduate students pretended to be participants in a ficticious affirmative action scenario. Results showed that when the participants pretended to be in a position in which they were selected due to preference, they reported negative reactions that have implications from a number of variables such as general affect and perception of fairness. In another study, by Nacoste and Lehman (1987), female undergraduate students were placed in simulated scenarios in which variables such as the person's qualifications and the selection procedure were manipulated. Results showed that when the participants believed they were selcted due to an unfair preference procedure, it increased the negative feelings of stigmatization.

Heilman has also looked at this question in a number of studies (for example, Heilman & Alcott, 2001; Heilman, Simon, & Repper, 1987). In one study, Heilman, Simon, and Repper (1987) again used a leader paradigm methodology similar to the one used in previous studies by Jacobson and Koch (1977) and, as I have described, by Heilman, Battle, Keller, and Lee (1998). Not surprisingly, Heilman's findings confirmed previous research which suggests that the self-image and self-evaluation of women was negatively affected by their knowledge that they were selected purely on the basis of gender preference. In a series of experimental studies by Heilman and Alcott (2001), which I reviewed earlier, about the effects of preferential selection on performance, Heilam also looked at the effects of preferential selection on self-regard and self-evaluation. Once again, she concluded that if the female participants believed it was known that they were selected because of gender preferences, it would have a negative psychological effect.

However, just like in the case of performance, most of these studies look at preference in an isolated, simple laboratory way that eliminates the interaction with real-life variables and situations. No study, for example, has compared the negative psychological effects of preferential treatment versus the effects of being outright rejected from a needed job, a promotion, or an academic institution. (I suspect people in those circumstances should feel pretty bad too.) Nevertheless, there have been a number of studies that attempted to account for other important mediating variables when looking at the effects of affirmative action on self-image, self-esteem, or self-evaluation.

In one of these studies, Stewart and Shapiro (2000) replicated and built on the original study by Heilman and her colleagues (1987). Undergraduate students from a multiethnic sample participated in an experiment in which they were told they were selected due to preference or merit. Stewart and Shapiro not only failed to find a negative effect on self-evaluation of women, but actually found that the African American participants in the preference group reported higher leadership scores. They explain this finding precisely because of a mechanism that helps stigmatized minorities in maintaining positive self-esteem. In other words, African American participants were set to "prove wrong" the conception that their performance would be lower than that of White participants.

In another study (Major, Feinstein, & Crocker, 1994) that followed the leadership paradigm methodology, participants believed they were selected either solely on the basis of preference, solely due to merit, or because of a combination of merit plus preference, which, as I mentioned before, more closely resembles a real affirmative action situation. Although Major and her colleagues replicated the results found by Heilman and her colleagues (1987) in the gender-only preference condition, they did not find any significant deleterious effects for the women on the preference plus merit condition.

A study by Brutus and Ryan (1998) confirms that allowing the beneficiary to include a perception that the selection was partly done on the basis of qualifications and not only because of preference alleviates the negative psychological effects of preferential treatment. Brutus and Ryan looked specifically at the concept of self-efficacy. They refer to Albert Bandura's (1986) definition of the term, which is "people's judgment of their capabilities to organize and execute courses of action required to attain designated types of perform-ances" (p. 391). In other words, how capable a person is believed to be in any certain area. Female students were divided into three groups to perform a complex mathematical task. In the first group, they were told that they were selected based on their merit. The second group believed they were selected solely because of their gender, a "direct preferential treatment" condition. Finally, in the third group, they re-ceived ambiguous information regarding their selection, a condition Brutus and Ryan refer to as "indirect preferential treatment" and which is more similar to what actually happens in real affirmative ac-tion situations. What Brutus and Ryan found was that when the op-erationalization of preferential treatment is done in an ambiguous, indirect way, not only did the participants with high pretask levels of self-efficacy perform better than the ones selected purely by merit, but the self-efficacy level of the women in the indirect group actually *in-creased* overall.

Taylor (1994) conducted the first comprehensive study that actu-ally looked at the psychological effects of affirmative action in real employment situations. By using data from the General Social Survey, as well as a number of psychological outcome measures, he found no negative effects whatsoever in any social psychological outcome for the people employed through affirmative action. In fact, a recent ex-tensive review of the literature (Truax et al., 1998) concluded that even though there is evidence of some negative psychological effects on beneficiaries in experimental studies with undergraduate students, the empirical evidence consistently shows that affirmative action has no deleterious effects in actual employment situations.

Another study performed with actual employees was conducted by Graves and Powell (1994). They mailed surveys to 188 male and female MBA graduates. Among other questions, they were asked to indicate if they believed they benefited from affirmative action poli-cies, as well as a number of questions related to their job satisfaction. The results indicated that the women in the study did not report any relation between the belief they benefited from gender preferences and their job satisfaction.

In summary, although the early evidence supported a possible effect of affirmative action on the psyche of the beneficiaries (includ-ing self-concept, self-esteem, self-efficacy, and job satisfaction), research that accounted for more complex interactions or that looked directly at real job situations was unable to find any evidence supporting this claim.

Conclusion

Looking at affirmative action from an objective perspective, we have to conclude that even though it has some drawbacks, these negative effects can be easily remedied. In addition, it is clear that affirmative action has had some major successes. In light of this evidence, it would not make sense, based on the "side effects," to consider eliminating affirmative action since the benefits seem to far outweigh the risks. Still, as Patterson (1998) wrote, affirmative action is supposed to be a self-canceling program that would no longer be needed when the ethnic and gender inequalities are eliminated. Therefore, although it should be concluded that affirmative action does not have to be eliminated on the basis of its negative effects, it should disappear on the basis of its success. Therefore, it is fair to ask Has affirmative action acomplished its goals? If we were to eliminate affirmative action today, would we find a fair and equal society, or would we go back to the days of rampant discrimination? Furthermore, is affirmative action currently our only alternative in minimizing the effects of latent stereotypes and prejudice in society? I will explore these questions in the next chapters.

Chapter 4

Affirmative Action and the Politics of Stereotype

Are stereotypes, prejudice, and discrimination still prevalent in American thinking of the twenty-first century? If so, do they affect the social and political issues regarding race and affirmative action in America? Let me tell you a short personal story. One of the reasons I became interested in the study of stereotypes is because although I am Mexican American, I also happen to be Jewish and blond with blue eyes, a fact that created quite a bit of dissonance in people who had a hard time boxing me into a stereotype. When I was first applying to graduate school, I went to New England for an interview at a top Ivy League university. I was flying first to New York, and then taking the train to the small town where this university is located. I spoke on the phone with a professor, a social psychologist who is one of the top experts in stereotypes, who was supposed to pick me up at the train station. As you can imagine, she was expecting a Mexican American fellow. I, on the other hand, was expecting to see a "professor." When I say I was expecting to see a professor, what I mean is a person at least in her mid- to late forties, with glasses, and a serious, respected look (sort of a cross between Janet Reno and Dr. Ruth). As I disembarked and people began to leave the station, I was puzzled. I did not see anyone who looked like a professor. Finally, there was no one left on the platform but a young woman, dressed in jeans and a T-Shirt, and me. Since there was no one else left, I concluded that it was possible that the professor could not come, and she sent a graduate student to pick me up instead. I approached her and asked, "Are you with the office of professor so and so?" "Yes," she said, "I am Professor so and so! Are you Mr. Salinas?" "Yes," I replied. "Oh, but you don't look Mexican," she muttered. "Well," I said, "you don't look like a professor either."

To answer if stereotypes, prejudice, and discrimination are still prevalent in American thinking, we should begin by looking at how psychology defines these terms.

What You Know (Stereotypes)

As you can see from my little anecdote, stereotypes are mental constructs that affect everyone, even national experts on the study of stereotypes. This is not surprising, though, because even though only recently we have discovered that some of our stereotypes are activated in an automatic, unconscious manner, the use of these unconscious stereotypes to judge and categorize people is as old as ancient civilization.

In the context of social sciences, however, the word *stereotype* was first used by the journalist Walter Lippman in 1922 (Stroebe & Insko, 1989) to refer to rigid, permanent mental images of various social groups. Stereotypes did not make their formal debut in the area of psychology until the widely known study by Katz and Braly (1933) in which they asked a group of college students to select, from a list, a number of traits that were most representative of ten different ethnic groups in the United States.

Contrary to its popular notion, the term *stereotype* was not automatically associated with a negative connotation. Lippman (1922) himself saw stereotypes as a means to set order on otherwise confusing ideas, and Harding and associates (Harding, Kutner, Proshansky, & Chein, 1954; Harding, Proshansky, Kutner, & Chein, 1969) believed that stereotypes were only the cognitive component of a three-component model of attitude formation (cognitive, affective, and behavioral), and therefore had no inherent, either negative or positive, affective value. More important, Harding differentiated between stereotypes, which he considered neutral, and prejudice, which is defined as a predominantly *negative* attitude toward members of some out-group (I will discuss prejudice later).

Even though prejudice sounds like a very important area to study, according to Duckitt (1992), the research of stereotypes and prejudice as part of social psychology was very limited until the 1940s. Only after World War II and the Holocaust in Europe did the interest in stereotype research increase dramatically (Fairchild & Gurin, 1978), reaching its highest point in 1954 with the publication of Gordon Allport's classic *The Nature of Prejudice*. Nevertheless, at this point, prejudice and stereotypical thinking were assumed to be linked to pathological personality and maladjustment of the individual (see, for example, Adorno, Frenkel-Brunswick, Levinson, & Sanford, 1950; Rokeach, Smith, & Evans, 1960; Smith & Rosen, 1958). It was not until the mid-1960s, mostly because of the influence of the civil rights movement, that the emphasis on stereotype research moved away from individual-level psychopathological approaches to a more sociocultural perspective that regarded stereotypes as social issue (Maluso, 1995). However, the period from the mid-1960s to the late 1970s was once again marked by a lack of interest in the research of stereotypes and prejudice (Duckitt, 1992).

Nevertheless, we saw the development of many important theories during that period, among them the Realistic Conflict Theory (Campbell, 1965; Sherif, 1967) and the Social Identity Theory (Tajfel, 1970, 1982; Tajfel & Turner, 1979) of stereotypes and prejudice. Although they differ in many ways, both theories saw the development of stereotypes and prejudice as a function of sociocultural factors and intergroup relations.

The Realistic Conflict Theory conceptualizes prejudice and stereotypes as the result of competition between groups for a scarce resource, a "[r]eal conflict of interest . . . [that] causes the perception of threat" (Campbell, 1965, p. 287). Campbell suggests that this perception of threat (whether real or imaginary) affects the attitudes of the members of the group toward the competing group, and also toward themselves, generating a sense of solidarity and ethnocentrism. These ideas were challenged by Tajfel's Social Identity Theory (Tajfel, 1970, 1982; Tajfel & Turner, 1979), which argued that conflict of interest does not necessarily lead to prejudice and stereotypes. Moreover, Tajfel and Turner (1979) argued that the presence of conflict is not even a necessary condition for in-group bias and ethnocentrism to occur. Their research suggested that the mere perception of belonging to a group is enough to produce in-group favoritism and intergroup discrimination. The Social Identity Theory proposes that stereotypes and prejudice are the result of an attempt to achieve a strong social identity by increasing the intergroup differentiation between in-group and out-group.

By the early 1980s, two factors prompted a paradigm shift in the field of stereotype research: On one hand, the available empirical evidence suggested that stereotypes could not be fully explained in terms of sociocultural and group structure factors. On the other hand, research on cognition, prompted by the cognitive revolution that was taking place in the social sciences, suggested that the formation of stereotypes was a more natural, cognitive process whose function was to simplify the complexity of the social environment (Ashmore & Del Boca, 1981) and therefore a process that is quite automatic and almost inevitable.

Presently, the field of stereotype research is dominated by cognitive-based models. Two main approaches can be identified in recent reviews of the literature: The social cognitive perspective and the cognitive motivational perspective (Duckitt, 1992; Hilton & Von Hippel, 1996; Lott & Maluso, 1995). The social cognitive perspective focuses on the investigation of the function of basic cognitive structures in affecting information processing and social behavior, and includes models such as the Nonconscious Detection of Covariation (Hill, Lewicki, Czyzewska, & Schuller, 1990; Hill, Lewicki, & Neubauer, 1991) and the Illusory Correlation (Hamilton & Sherman, 1989; Mullen & Johnson, 1990). In contrast, the cognitive motivational perspective considers social categorization as the trigger to motivational processes to evaluate one's group more positively than the out-group, and includes such models as the Belief Congruence Theory (Insko, Nacoste, & Moe, 1983; Rokeach et al., 1960) and the Social Identity Theory (Tajfel, 1982; Tajfel & Turner, 1979).

Contemporary theorists have been attempting to develop more integrated models of stereotype formation and change that are more congruent with the older models of the 1970s and the recent empirical findings of the 1990s (Hilton & Von Hippel, 1996). These findings suggest that stereotypes are not only mental devices that ease information processing (by allowing the individual to access previous knowledge instead of incoming information), but emerge as the result of environmental and contextual factors (see, for example, Eagly, 1995; Fiske, 1993; Kruglanski & Webster, 1996).

Today, stereotypes are no longer seen as rigid overgeneralizations or mental images. Modern definitions of stereotypes regard them not only as beliefs about the characteristics and behaviors of individuals belonging to certain groups, but also as "theories about how and why certain attributes go together" (Hilton & Von Hippel, 1996, p. 238). According to Hilton & Von Hippel (1996), the nature and purpose of these individual theories play a major role in defining when and where stereotypes are activated and likely to change.

Are Stereotypes Affecting Political Attitudes?

Are stereotypes affecting both the debate and the decision-making process in issues related to race, such as affirmative action, welfare, and crime? After reviewing the theories on stereotypes, the answer to that question has to be an unequivocal yes. In the late 1980s to mid-1990s, as a profusion of cognitive research on stereotypes was taking place, it became increasingly clear that stereotypes have a pretty much involuntary, automatic component that is activated regardless of the level of prejudice of a person (see, for example, Devine, 1989; Lepore & Brown, 1997). In a landmark paper, Patricia Devine (1989) reported a series of studies that supported a theoretical model that separated stereotypes and prejudice in controlled and automatic components. In one study, Devine administered a prejudice questionnaire to a group of undergraduate students, and based on that score, placed them into either a high-prejudiced or low-prejudiced group. Then she divided the participants in both groups again. To half of them she showed, for a fraction of a second, words that were associated with the African American stereotype, like lazy and violent. To the other half she showed neutral words. Finally, she asked the participants to read a story about a man of unspecified ethnicity who was behaving in an ambiguous way that could be interpreted either positively or negatively. What Devine found was that the participants who were presented with the stereotypical words, regardless of the level of prejudice, tended to interpret the man's behavior in a more negative way than the ones who saw the neutral words. In other words, the automatic component of the stereotype was activated unconsciously in all participants.

In these studies, Devine found strong evidence that regardless of the level of prejudice a person has toward an out-group, not only do both, low- and high-prejudiced people, have comparable knowledge of the stereotype, but the automatic component of the stereotype is equally activated in them when the individual is presented with a stereotype-relevant stimulus (anything from meeting a member of the stereotyped group or reading a paragraph regarding that group to being exposed to more subtle symbols such as music or cultural artifacts). Furthermore, these studies indicate that low-prejudiced individuals actually required purposeful *inhibition* of the stereotype in order to control the stereotype, which suggests that stereotyping might be the more "natural" response, while controlling it requires conscious effort.

Although it is important to note that other researchers have found that the automatic component of racial stereotypes is activated differently for low-prejudiced and high-prejudiced people, and under different circumstances (see, for example, Fazio, Jackson, & Dunton, 1995; Lepore & Brown, 1997), there is broad consensus that, regardless of our level of prejudice, stereotypes would be activated if we are exposed to situations that are racially charged, such as talking about affirmative action, welfare reform, immigration, and crime rates. In other words, even for low-prejudice people, it is very likely that stereotypes will play some role when discussing issues that are racially charged.

Specifically, a number of studies have shown a connection between racial beliefs, stereotypes, and policy attitudes. For example, Gilens (1995) studied if racial stereotyping affects White people's position on welfare. He found that racial attitudes are a more important factor in predicting opposition to welfare than economic self-interest, individualism, or egalitarianism. He concluded that contrary to the conventional wisdom that ethnic prejudice is no longer an important factor in American politics, the stereotype of African Americans as lazy is not only widespread but still has a significant effect on the political debate.

Bobo and Kluegel (1993) used data from the General Social Survey conducted in 1990 to review the connection between attitudes toward social programs in general and racial stereotypes and prejudice in particular. This is an extensive survey in which about thirteen hundred American adults were interviewed on a variety of social issues. Bobo and Kluegel found that the level of opposition toward social policies increased significantly when the policy was presented as explicitly targeting African Americans, suggesting that opposition to the social assistance policies is very often the result of racial and ethnic attitudes instead of principled opposition to the policy itself.

Similarly, Hurwitz and Peffley (1997) used a technique called "Computer Assisted Telephone Interviewing" (CATI) which allows the manipulation of variables during telephone interviews. They called more than two thousand adults to ask about attitudes regarding crime policy. In one of the conditions, the participants were asked their opinion about punishment for violent crimes, but the questionnaire varied randomly to present a perpetrator who was White or African American. They found that when the survey was formulated under the condition in which the criminal was African American, the attitudes of the participants tended to significantly favor tougher and more punitive penalties than when the criminal was White. Although Hurwitz and Peffley concluded that the effect of race attitudes was significant only when the crimes were violent and when the policies were punitive, they still concluded that, since these are circumstances usually linked to crimes, people's opinions in this area are undoubtedly influenced by racial attitudes.

In a different study, Peffley and Hurwitz (1998) use again the CATI technique to conduct a survey regarding attitudes toward welfare. They asked the participants if they supported welfare programs that were either "specially designed to help blacks" (p. 82) or "new immigrants from Europe" (p. 82). By doing a statistical procedure known as "multiple regression," which connects the responses to these questions with other survey answers regarding stereotypes, attitudes, and demography, Peffley and Hurwitz found a significant relationship between stereotypes and prejudice against African Americans and opposition to ethnically targeted welfare programs. They plainly concluded that "clearly, when whites evaluate welfare for black—but not immigrant—recipients, their decision to support welfare is heavily colored by racial stereotypes" (p. 82). In the same paper, Peffley and Hurwitz reported another study, which is similar to the welfare study in structure but this time the question was related to a drug search:

Now, consider an instance where the police see two young [African American, White] men about 20 years old. They are [using foul language, are well dressed, and are well behaved] and walking very near a house where the police know drugs are being sold. The police search them and find that they are carrying drugs. Do you think this is definitely a reasonable search? (p. 87)

Peffley and Hurwitz found once more, using multiple regression, that the stereotypes and attitudes of White people toward African Americans heavily influenced their support for the search of the African American suspects as reasonable. These results are further supported in a study by Carmines and Layman (1998) which found that negative stereotypes of African Americans significantly correlates with opposition to Equal Opportunity and Affirmative Action programs. (Ironically, although significant correlations were found for all—Republican, Independent, and Democrat—participants in the study, the most and strongest correlations were found among Democrats.)

In another example, Dovidio, Smith, Donnella, and Gaertner (1997) researched the relationship between prejudice and death penalty sentencing of African Americans and Whites. In their study, participants read an account of the same trial, except in half of the cases the accused was African American and in the other half the accused was White. Then, the participant watched a video of five "jurors," which could be either all White or four White and one African American, in which they explain their decision to vote for capital punishment. Then, participants completed a questionnaire in which they expressed their own opinion regarding the sentencing. Dovidio and his colleagues found that people with higher levels of prejudice were a lot more likely to recommend the death penalty for the African American defendant. Interestingly enough, people with low levels of prejudice were also more likely to support capital punishment for the African American defendant if one of the "jurors" was African American. Apparently, seeing an African American juror supporting the death penalty releases the White participants from a stigma of prejudice, and therefore they feel free to support it themselves.

Another study looked at the relationship of stereotypes and prejudice and attitudes toward undocumented migrant workers from Mexico (Lee, Ottati, & Hussain, 2001). This study was conducted in California in the wake of Proposition 187, which essentially deprived undocumented workers from most government services, including education, health, and welfare. The researchers conducted a study with college students in which they assessed their support/opposition for Proposition 187, as well as a number of items related to stereotypes and prejudice toward Mexicans. The researchers found a significant correlation between stereotypes and support for Proposition 187. The study yielded results which support, once more, that attitudes and prejudice against an ethnic group (in this case, Mexican Americans) strongly influenced the individual's support or opposition to ethnically related social policy.

Finally, there is one more general example of the effects of stereotypes in the political debate that I would like to mention. Tedin (1994) studied the issue of education and racial/ethnic equality. Tedin had a rare opportunity to use a real-life situation in which the circumstances naturally divide the players into experimental and control groups, a situation some refer to as a "natural experiment." In this case, because of court-mandated financial redistribution of resources, some school districts stood to have a decrease in their funding while others stood to gain funds. Tedin surveyed the families involved in both types of districts in a number of variables, including racial beliefs (stereotypes). He found that even though self-interest was the most important predictor of support or opposition to the fund redistribution, symbolic beliefs associated with race were still a significant predictor. This study is particularly relevant because, unlike other "simulated situation" studies in which the opinion of the participant is not really related to real-life consequences, in this case the racial attitudes were directly related to a very real school funding issue.

Affirmative Action and Stereotypes

As I have shown, there are some strong theoretical models and there is plenty of empirical evidence supporting the thesis that stereotypes, and in many cases, outright prejudice, influence the attitudes and opinions of Americans when it comes to racially and ethnically related social policies. However, this book deals specifically with affirmative action, and therefore I have left the research specific to affirmative action for this section.

There are a number of studies that have found a relationship between stereotypes and prejudice and support for affirmative action. In one recent study, Federico and Sidanius (2002), using data from National Election Studies of 1986 and 1992, found that among

White respondents political ideology and ethnic policy attitudes were closely associated with beliefs of ethnic equality/superiority, and that egalitarian beliefs predicted support for affirmative action and equal opportunity.

In another investigation, Bobocel, Davey, Son Hing, and Zanna (2001) conducted a series of four studies to determine whether justice concerns are a legitimate reason to oppose affirmative action, or if they only serve as an excuse for rationalizing negative beliefs and prejudice against minorities. They conducted extensive interviews with undergraduate students, asking about support for or opposition against affirmative action, as well as a number of questions about stereotypes, prejudice, and racial beliefs. Although Bobocel and her colleagues concluded that for some individuals, justice concerns can be a valid reason to oppose affirmative action, they also found that prejudiced people tend to oppose the application of affirmative action under the pretext that it is unjust, even when most other people see this application as fair.

Little, Murry, and Wimbush (1998) conducted another study in which they investigated whether self-esteem and prejudice influence people's support for affirmative action programs in the workplace. They gave a questionnaire to over seven hundred undergraduate students to measure self-esteem and symbolic prejudice, as well as demographic variables and support for affirmative action. Results of the study showed that both high prejudice and low self-esteem predict opposition to affirmative action in the workplace.

Another example is a study by Williams, Jackson, Brown, Torres, Forman, and Brown (1999) that investigated if racial prejudice predicted different levels of support for affirmative action in particular and other government programs to help African Americans in general. In this study, more than eleven hundred White adults were surveyed about different factors affecting support for ethnically oriented social policies including racial prejudice and self-interest. This study is of special relevance because of all the factors that were included in the survey, the authors found that prejudice was the most important predictor of support/opposition to affirmative action and social policies.

Finally, a study by James, Brief, Dietz, and Cohen (2001) explored the effects of affirmative action policies on Whites' job-related attitudes. James and her colleagues conducted an extensive survey about job satisfaction and promotion opportunities, as well as racial attitudes. They found that the level of prejudice of the participants affected in a considerable manner both their perception of the fairness of the affirmative action and equal employment opportunity programs in their own organizations, as well as their level of satisfaction with opportunities for promotion within their own organizations.

Are Stereotypes Still Prevalent?

What most of this research suggests so far is that people's prejudices and stereotypes shape their opinion and support for racially oriented social programs in general and affirmative action in particular. Specifically, people who are highly prejudiced or hold racial stereotypes tend to oppose such programs. Now, although this conclusion should be enough to support the thesis that prejudice and stereotypes are influencing the debate and the political process when it comes to social issues, this would not be so harmful if the level of prejudice and overt stereotyping were low and examples of prejudice and discrimination were few and far between. Unfortunately, that is not the case. Although overt ethnic stereotypes of minorities have declined in the past few decades (see, for example, Sigelman & Tuch, 1997), several studies have found that more "passive" negative stereotypes are quite prevalent. Devine and Elliot (1995), in an empirical study, reviewed and retested some of the cornerstone studies regarding racial stereotypes that support the notion of a "fading" racial stereotype, known as "The Princeton Trilogy." Devine and Elliot concluded that contrary to the idea that stereotypes are waning, a consistent negative stereotype of African Americans still exists, except it has taken a more subtle, contemporary form.

For example, in a review of several national surveys of ethnic stereotypes, Smith (1991, 2001) found that Whites still unproportionately perceive African Americans as unintelligent, aggressive, poor, and lazy. Hudson and Hines-Hudson (1999), in an extensive study of contemporary racial attitudes, concluded that "the values and behaviors of both Whites and African Americans in the sample were influenced powerfully by attitudes grounded in centuries old racial stereotypes" (p. 22). Similarly, Peffley (1994) reported that 31 percent of White Americans responding to a national survey still considered African Americans to be lazy and 50 percent considered them aggressive.

This trend is also observable in opinion surveys reported in the general media. In one poll of nearly three thousand people nation-wide conducted by Louis Harris Research in mid-1993 and reported in the *Detroit Free Press* (Goldberg, 1994), 21 percent of Whites (as well as 31 percent of Asian Americans and 26 percent of Latinos) agreed that African Americans "want to live on welfare." In addition, about 50 percent of Whites and African Americans and 68 percent of Asian Americans believed that Latinos "tend to have bigger families than they are able to support."

Another shocking survey, this one conducted by the Opinion Re-search Center at the University of Chicago and reported in *The Christian Science Monitor* ("U.S.," 1991), also found stereotypes to be quite ubiquitous. It found that 62 percent of White respondents be-lieve that African Americans are lazier than Whites, 56 percent that they are more violence prone than Whites, and 53 percent think they are less intelligent. Also, 55 percent of non-Hispanic Whites indicated that Latinos were less intelligent than Whites. In addition, 78 percent of White respondents believe African Americans are more likely to choose living off welfare benefits than Whites. Stereotypes are also widespread among minorities. According to this survey, 50 percent of people from non-Hispanic minorities surveyed believed that Latinos are more prone to violence than Whites and close to 75 percent be-lieve they are more likely to prefer to live off welfare.

Other surveys have supported the notion that stereotypes are just as common among minorities as they are among Whites. In 1994, Harris conducted a survey of the stereotypes of minorities in the United States. Participants were surveyed about White stereotypes, and 66 percent believed Whites to be insensitive to other people, as well as having a long history of racism and prejudice. In addition, 65 percent responded that Whites believe they are superior, and 61 per-cent believe that Whites do not want to share power and wealth with non-Whites. Harris concluded that "minorities suspect the worst about White America: that it is made up of people who are both in-sensitive and uncaring about non-whites" (p. 665).

The pervasiveness of stereotypes in America is not surprising, since stereotypes are very common and highly visible in American culture during the late twentieth and early twenty-first centuries. For example, racial stereotypes plague the quintessential American cultural medium, television. According to the Children Now Foundation in their annual "Fallcolors" report of prime-time television characters for 2001–2002, minorities are represented in prime-time television programs in highly stereotypical ways. The foundation reports that, for example:

- Among major recurring characters, criminals, service workers or unskilled laborers were only portrayed by minorities.
- Nearly 50 percent of Hispanic characters held positions or occupations generally considered to be lower status.
- Few Native Americans are featured in prime time (none of them women) and when they do, they tend to play the role of spiritual adviser or healer.
- In the 8–9 p.m. slot (when children are most likely to watch), 61 percent of all major characters in any given program were all white or all black, as opposed to only 16 percent that had a diverse opening-credit cast.

Furthermore, these stereotypical minority characters are not only prevalent in television, but they can also be seen in films, where according to Long (2002), portrayals of minority characters are usually consistent with social stereotypes.

This blatant display of stereotypical portrayals of minorities in our major cultural vehicles is troubling enough as it is. However, it is even worse because recent research suggests that media stereotypes have an influence on the actual opinions and views of people regarding race and social programs. One model, proposed by Tan, Fujioka, and Tan (2000), has received empirical support for explaining how television stereotypes affect people's perceptions of minorities, which in turn affect their opinions regarding government racially oriented social policy. In this study, they questioned 166 White undergraduate students, and found that their perceptions of stereotypical television characters was correlated to actual racial stereotypes, which in turn was related to their opposition to affirmative action. In other words, some people *believe* the stereotypical characterizations they see on television as being real, and their opinions regarding social policies are then shaped by these fictional characterizations.

More evidence that the ethnic portrayals of the mass media are influencing peoples stereotypes can be found in a 2001 survey conducted by Zogby International for the National Italian American

Foundation. In this poll of over twelve hundred teenagers, 31 percent of respondents who watch television frequently identified "Being a gang member" as a typical characteristic of African Americans, and 27 percent said it was one of Hispanics. Other stereotypes were also reinforced: 34 percent said "Being a Terrorist" is a typical characteristic of Arabs, 44 percent identified Italian Americans as "Crime Bosses," and 26 percent identified the Irish as "Drunkards."

Stereotypes are not only prevalent in our media and our public opinion, but they also shape our judgment and behavior, often in the unconscious, automatic manner described earlier in this chapter. A number of classical studies have found a connection between our nonconscious stereotypes and not only our attitudes, but our *behavior* toward the stereotyped groups.

In one study by Duncan (1976) about one hundred White participants watched a videotape of two men having an argument. The two men were actors performing the exact same script, one was White, the other African American. In one version, the White participant slightly shoves the African American one, while in the other the roles are reversed. When the White participant shoved the African American, only 13 percent of the participants perceived the act as "violent." However, when the African American man shoved the White man, 73 percent qualified the act as violent.

In another classic study, this one by Coates (1972), undergraduate students had to teach White and African American nine-year-old children a verbal task. Coates found not only that the male undergraduates behaved more negatively toward the African American children than toward the White children during the teaching assignment, but that both male and female teachers rated African American children more negatively on their performance even though the performance data provided to the undergraduates was not real and was made to be equivalent across race.

Other more contemporary studies have replicated these patterns. For example, Sbarra and Pianta (2001) found that kindergarten and first grade teachers rate African American children higher in behavior problems and lower in competency; and Pigott and Cowen (2000), in a comprehensive survey of kindergarten to fifth grade teachers, found that African American students were judged by their teachers as having more stereotypically negative characteristics and serious school adjustment problems than White children, while at the same time being less competent. Teachers also predicted that African American children would have a poorer educational future.

Although it is quite unsettling to see these attitudes prevail in schools, these beliefs and behaviors, of course, go beyond the classroom setting. For example, Simpson and Strong (1986) performed an elegant experiment in which participants were "paired" with an either African American or White confederate. Each pair had a task to complete, but in half of the pairs the participant was placed in charge, while on the other half, the confederate was. The study found that when a White participant was in charge of an African American confederate, the White participant tended to have a poor opinion of and to derogate the African American confederate. However, if the confederate was White, the tendency was to praise them.

Implications of these studies are quite obvious in real-life situations, since we are more likely to believe and support situations that conform to our social stereotypes than those that contradict them. One example was the case of Susan Smith, who in 1994 murdered her two young sons by drowning them in a lake in South Carolina. At first, Mrs. Smith told police that an African American man had abducted her children. Although the police later declared that they never believed Mrs. Smith's story, they nevertheless proceeded to conduct a massive nine-day manhunt for the African American carjacker, and a national outcry arose that African American residents of the town of Union, South Carolina, as well as national African American leaders, deeply resented ("Blacks," 1994; "Trouble," 1995).

This situation is similar to the 1989 case of Charles Stuart, a Boston businessman who became the object of nationwide sympathy after he claimed an African American man shot his pregnant wife in the head point-blank. Stuart's allegations, which were later proven false, set off a police dragnet that not only deepened Boston's already volatile racial tensions at the time (African American leaders complained of police harassment), but resulted in the arrest of William Bennett, an innocent man.

What these two stories have in common is how easy it is to play on a racial stereotype to get the public, the press, and law enforcement worked up. In both cases, Mrs. Smith and Mr. Stuart, the perpetrators of horrible crimes, played on the stereotypes of ethnic minorities to deflect blame, which is not surprising. What is remarkable, is the social and political reaction that the activation of the stereotype produced at all levels. Probably none of the players in these stories considered themselves prejudiced or racist. Yet their behaviors were clearly influenced by the stereotype elicited of the images of young African American men committing terrible crimes against White people.

Another example of how our stereotypes affect our perceptions, beliefs, and political support can be observed in an article in *The Washington Post* that appeared in July 2002. The headline of the article reads: "To Revive Agenda, Bush Courts African Americans; Support Sought for Welfare Reform, 'Faith-Based' Charity, Home-ownership" (p. A8). The article reports about a campaign appearance that George Bush made at an African American church in Cleveland, Ohio, in which he touted his welfare reform and education initiatives. He proceeded to frame these issues in terms of their benefits for minorities with statements such as "the percentage of single black mothers working is the highest ever and poverty amongst black children is the lowest ever" and "It's easy to walk into a classroom full of inner-city African Americans, for example, and say, 'You can't learn, we'll move you through'" (p. A8). Although his statements cannot be characterized as prejudiced in any respect, he is framing the political debate in terms that reaffirm the social stereotypes. Otherwise, why did he select a campaign appearance with a predominantly African American audience to talk about welfare and school vouchers? Although we would hope that Mr. Bush does not share this stereotype, it is clear that his selection of welfare as *the* appropriate campaign issue to discuss when he visits an African American church in Middle America reflects the connection between the stereotype and the policy.

Some social commentators and academicians are not even willing to give the politics of stereotype the benefit of the doubt that automatic, subconscious processing would entail. For example, Pat Swift (1998), of *The Buffalo News* draws into the connection between race and politics in the issue of welfare. He claims that the whole welfare reform movement of the mid- to late 1990s is the result of "racially driven public policy" (p. 7C) because a program that was originally set up to help White mothers during the depression, came under attack only when "more women of color sought the same assistance" (p. 7C). Swift cites Professor Lucy Williams, from Northeastern University, who believes racism is an underlying factor in the welfare reform movement. Williams claims the Conservative Right's campaign to link welfare programs to issues such as immorality, unemployment, crime, and teen pregnancy connected the issue to race, and although statistics show that the typical welfare recipient is a White female with an average of two children, the stereotype of the welfare recipient became that of a teenage minority woman who takes advantage of welfare to have more and more children out of wedlock.

What About the Future?

I have talked quite a bit about the relationship between stereotypes and political beliefs. These stereotypes, however, are just beliefs that would be nothing more than academic curiosities if they did not have an actual affect on our behavior. As I discussed earlier in this chapter, behavior that is consciously driven by stereotypes is called "prejudice." Laws and programs designed to prevent this type of behavior, such as Affirmative Action, Equal Employment Opportunity, and the American with Disabilities Act, can sometimes make it more difficult to observe the latent attitudes of people in society by preventing the display of the overt prejudiced behavior. This, however, does not mean that the attitudes have disappeared, just that they are hidden. Therefore, it is fair to ask, absent affirmative action, Would we go back to the days of rampant inequalities in hiring and admissions practices?

It is clear that, as the legal experiences in California and Texas have shown, the end of affirmative action would have significant consequences in education and employment in the short term. I have reviewed numerous examples of precipitous declines in minority enrollment in top public universities in Texas and California. However, a couple more are appropriate in order to recapitulate. According to Bob Laird (2002), in October 1998, the first year after the end of affirmative action in enrollment in California, only about 9 percent of UC–Berkeley's enrolled freshman class was African American, Chicano, or Native American, compared to 19.1 percent in the fall 1997 semester. The 9 percent number is even more striking when we consider that the original number of 19 percent was inadequate to begin with (about 40 percent of the California high school graduating class were underrepresented minorities). The numbers are even more appalling in the elite schools of law in California: In 2000, at the University of California–Los Angeles (UC–Los Angeles), only 5 out of a class of 305 were African American; at UC–Berkeley, only 7 out of a class of 270 were African American; and at UC–Davis, only 2 out of a class of 168 were African American (Parloff, 2002).

Some commentators, however, suggest that this is just the tip of the iceberg. For example, Hutchinson (1997) sees only an increase in prejudice as conservatives push forward an agenda of a supposedly color-blind society that does not differentiate people based on their race. He claims that they still hold a "litany of racial stereotypes and slanders" (p. 9) and cites examples in which they still support the misconceptions that "blacks are disproportionately unemployed (lazy), are underrepresented at colleges (stupid) and have fewer businesses (lack initiative and discipline)" (p. 9). Hutchinson further explains that a color-blind society will not be possible, and prejudice will be a dangerous reality, as long as White America does not fully realize and come to grips with the fact that Whites actually account for the majority of violent crime committed in America, as well as most of the illegal drug use and the majority of people living in poverty and receiving welfare. Also Feagin and Sikes (1994) bring forward evidence showing that despite laws prohibiting discrimination, professionals in fields such as banking, real estate, the hospitality industry, law enforcement, and even cab drivers find ways to "legally" circumvent the law and still be prejudiced in their occupations.

In fact, there is a great deal of research suggesting that even with the change to more contemporary stereotypes and all the programs to protect the employment of minorities, including affirmative action, subtle prejudice in employment is still prevalent (see, for example, Bento, 1997; Brugnoli, Campion, & Basen, 1979; Dovidio & Gaertner, 2000; Frazer & Wiersma, 2001; Hitt, Zikmund, & Pickens, 1982; McConahay, 1983; McRae, 1991; Moss & Tilly, 1996; Stewart & Perlow, 2001; Tomkiewicz, Brenner, & Adeyemi-Bello, 1998).

In one example, Stewart and Perlow (2001), a simulation was carried out in which 181 participants evaluated the employment qualifications of African American and White applicants. Participants that scored higher on a measure to determine negative racial attitudes were more confident if they decided to hire African American applicants for a low-status job and White applicants for a high-status one. Stewart and Perlow concluded that the results of the study suggest that there was an observable pattern of subtle discrimination at work.

In another example of how prejudice can affect employment decisions in subtle ways, Frazer and Wiersma (2001) had White undergraduate students review applications and then interview an African American or White confederate of the study, both of whom had been matched in qualifications, and who pretended to be applicants for the job. Right after the interview, the participants made hiring recommendations from both groups about equally. However, after one week, the participants who interviewed African American candidates remembered them to be significantly less intelligent than the ones who interviewed White applicants (in fact, both interviewees, since they were confederates of the studies, read from identical scripts).

Another study that found patterns of prejudice in hiring practices was conducted by Dovidio and Gaertner (2000). They compared samples of simulated hiring situations from 1989 with a new sample they conducted in 1999. Although they discovered that self-reported prejudice declined in the ten-year period, they also found that White participants in the 1999 study still tended to discriminate against African Americans when the difference in qualifications between African Americans and Whites was ambiguous.

All these studies were, in fact, simulations conducted under experimental, controlled conditions. However, can we see this same pattern of subtle prejudice in real-life situations? In one of the very few studies conducted with real personnel administrators (Hitt, Zikmund, & Pickens, 1982), identical fake resumes were sent to two hundred companies in which the only difference was that the applicant was identified as either African American or female in half of them, or left unidentified in the other half. Resumes in which the applicant was identified as African American received significantly fewer positive responses than the unidentified ones, suggesting once again a pattern of subtle prejudice.

From these studies, we can clearly conclude that even with the protections granted today by Affirmative Action and Equal Employment Opportunity laws, prejudice is still a problem in hiring. If these protections were to disappear, we cannot reasonably expect a color-blind pattern of hiring to emerge at this point.

Stereotype Threat

One last effect of the politics of stereotype, and the way they perpetuate racial and gender stigmas, is the effect these stereotypes can have on their targets. For example, does knowledge of the stereotype increase the probability that minorities would underperform in school, or even drop out?

The research in the field of stereotypes has mostly followed a unidirectional orientation; most of the efforts in the area have been aimed at developing models to explain the emergence of stereotypes on the "stereotyper," without considering the effects of these stereotypes on the victims of stigma. One of the few models that explains the effects of these stereotypes on stigmatized minorities was developed recently at Stanford University by Claude Steele and Joshua Aronson (1995), and is called "stereotype threat." Stereotype threat is defined as "being at risk of confirming, as self characteristic, a negative stereotype about one's group" (p. 797). The empirical data gathered at this point (see, for example, Aronson et al., 1999; Spencer, 1994; Spencer, Steele, & Brown, 1997; Steele & Aronson, 1995) strongly suggest that, when members of stigmatized minorities are in a situation in which they are aware of their "low academic achievement" stereotype (or "primed"), they present a sharp decline in their performance in academic tasks. These data support the basic assumptions of the stereotype threat model. For example, in their landmark 1995 study, Steele and Aronson showed how a subtle reminder of the well-known stereotype regarding African American intellectual inferiority aroused enough anxiety to negatively affect the performance of highly motivated and prepared African American college students (from Stanford University!) taking a standardized test. When the same testing situation was designed to minimize thoughts about the stereotype, the African American students performed as well as the White students taking the test. Not only does this reveal an important psychological consequence of stereotypes, but it also helps explain a contributing factor in the low academic performance of minorities.

There is some controversy regarding the breadth of the definition of the stereotype threat effect. On one hand, stereotype threat might be seen exclusively as the result of apprehension (due to the concern that the individual might confirm the negative stereotype of his or her group). On the other hand, it can be defined as a broader phenomenon that might include any effect on behavior due to the knowledge that there is a negative stereotype of one's own group. Steele and Aronson (1995) talk about stereotype threat as "the threat of possibly being judged and treated stereotypically, or of possibly self-fulfilling such stereotype" (p. 798). Furthermore, they do not limit the effect to the diminished performance of minorities on standardized academic tests, but they stress the fact that it can affect any individual with a group identity "about which some negative stereotype exists" (p. 798) and therefore can be connected to any stereotypical behavior, like violence, selfishness, and so on. In that context a number of assumptions can be made that represent necessary conditions for the stereotype threat effect to occur:

1. The individual has to identify himself or herself with a stigmatized group.
2. The person must be aware of this stigma.
3. The stereotype has to be relevant to a specific situation.
4. The individual is concerned that his or her outcome of this situation might be affected by the perceptions the person and/or others might have regarding this stereotype.
5. This concern affects in some way the person's behavior.

In this sense, stereotype threat might affect an individual by increasing his or her apprehension, for example, during a test, and therefore negatively affecting his or her performance. Alternatively, the individual might decide to withdraw effort because of a concern derived from the low-performance stereotype, a way of "dis-identifying" with the task as something they do not really care about.

Some of the latest studies on stereotype threat have shed light on its effect on the educational performance of minority students. For example, we know that targets of negative stereotypes can successfully protect their self-esteem by attributing negative feedback to prejudice (see, for example, Crocker & Major, 1989). In one study, Aronson, Steele, Salinas, and Lustina (1999) studied the role this attribution strategy may play in the underperformance of minorities on standardized tests. Mexican American and White college students were presented with two verbal sections on a GRE test. Midway through the test, half of the test takers were given a "demographic questionnaire" that reminded them about their attitudes regarding test bias by asking them to rate the "level of bias" as one of the reasons for the difficulty of the test. This reminder had a significantly deleterious effect on the subsequent performance of the Latino students, but no effect on that of the White students. Taken together with subsequent measures of self-esteem, these results suggest that thinking about the cultural bias associated with standardized tests can hinder the performance of minorities in these types of tests as a way of protecting their self-esteem.

As another consequence of stereotype threat, Claude Steele (1997) also suggested that these negative social stereotypes can frustrate the attempt of minority students to successfully identify with school. This lack of identification can lead to effort withdrawal, low academic achievement in general, and underperformance in standardized tests in particular. Recent research supports this model. Preliminary data from one study (Salinas & Aronson, 2002) suggests this effort withdrawal mechanism can also be a consequence of stereotype threat. This study was similar in design to a previous one (Aronson, Steele, Salinas, & Lustina, 1999) except participants completed a test anxiety and a "motivation" questionnaire at the end. The pattern of response in those questionnaires suggests that after being reminded of the cultural bias, the level of motivation and test anxiety of the students dropped, as well as their performance in the second half of the test.

Conclusion

Stereotypes, prejudice, and discrimination are definitely a latent danger that does not allow for a truly color-blind society to exist in America at this time. We can see how even with the legal, political, and social protections that exist today, the attitudes and behaviors of people in society are affected, and sometimes even shaped, by stereotypes. Weakening social programs that help fight and remediate the effects of this clear and present prejudice is definitely not a solution. However, as I also discussed, affirmative action as it exists today only compensates for discrimination and is far from addressing the root causes of discrimination: A system that is not only plagued by stereotypes, but that arbitrarily favors some cultural learning styles and definitions of merit that we rarely question and that have very little scientific support. Only a paradigm shift in the way we educate our children today can bring about, perhaps in a generation or two, the true change that can lead to a color-blind society and the end of affirmative action as we know it.

Chapter 5

A Learner-Centered Paradigm

Education either functions as an instrument which is used to fa-
cilitate the integration of the younger generation into the logic of
the present system and bring about conformity to it, or it be-
comes "the practice of freedom," the means by which men and
women deal critically and creatively with reality and discover
how to participate in the transformation of their world.
　　　　　—Richard Shaull, Introduction to Paulo Freire's
　　　　　　　　　　　　　　　　Pedagogy of the Oppressed

The school classroom did not always look the way it does today. For
all of us who remember old television series like *Little House on the*
Prairie, the old model of the "schoolhouse" in which several kids of
different ages working on different assignments and levels of instruction would look perhaps antiquated and inefficient, but not unfamil-
iar. In the mid-nineteenth century, however, with the industrial
revolution in full swing and the increased need for skilled workers, a
number of American thinkers, particularly Horace Mann, began to
propose a more efficient model of education that would be focused
on the utilitarian needs of the new industrial society: Training skilled
workers while at the same time acculturating the population into the
moral values of the capitalist, Western society (Nellen, 2001;
Schrenko, 1994). This model of education, known as the "factory

model," was introduced at the time as the guiding principle in American public education. First, it proposed to group all students in classrooms chronologically. Then, students were to learn the same material at the same time from the same textbook, and great emphasis would be placed on discipline and organization (Schrenko, 1994).

Although a factory model of education made sense for the emerging industrial society of the late nineteenth century, it is clear that there are some major issues that became patent in the educational experience of the twentieth century.

What Is Wrong with Education Today?

Every semester I ask my students a very simple question: What is the purpose, or ultimate goal, of K–12 education? The discussion that ensues is interesting, but, in fact, quite alarming. Most of my students are upper division teacher education majors attempting to get certification to teach in our public schools. Many of them are in their last semester, well into their internships working in various schools with children in different grades and of different ages. Moreover, even my graduate students are many times "seasoned" teachers who have been in the system for several years and are working to get a graduate degree for personal or administrative reasons. Yet, it is surprising how unclear it is for them what the objective of the system they are serving, or about to serve, is. Some of them will quickly answer that the goal is "to transfer knowledge." That would be just fine, except when I give them a quick quiz about some basic middle school–level material in history, geography, math, and physics, they realize that the vast majority of the knowledge they supposedly "acquired" in school is really not there. If transfer of knowledge is the ultimate goal of our school system, any educational program in which the vast majority of the knowledge is gone by the time the program is finished has to be considered at best as very inefficient, at worst, a colossal failure. The students even joke, ironically, about how they "aced" a particular test of which they remember absolutely nothing today.

The answer, of course, if we go back to Horace Mann, is that transfer of knowledge is *not* the goal of our public education system. Our schools started as utilitarian schools that were supposed to train future workers and consumers with the *skills* they needed to be productive members of society (more on this later). Other than the most basic skills of reading, writing, and basic arithmetic, everything else in the school curriculum does not necessarily have any intrinsic value to it, but serves only as a vehicle to acculturate and socialize our children into society (Kohn, 1999; Lamm, 1976).

However, as one of the most important principles of program evaluation states, the *assessment* of a program must match the *objectives* of such program (not to talk about the contents, techniques, and methodologies, of course). In other words, if socialization is the major goal of schooling, then its assessment methods, from grades to tests, should measure precisely that. It is no wonder, then, that most of my students are confused regarding the goal of schooling because they intuitively matched the content proficiency tests and grading system with the goal they assumed they reflect, transfer of knowledge. The same is true about the methods and content of our school's curriculum, they are a mishmash of the original purpose of utilitarian socialization with the lack of vision of many political programs (for example, "no child left behind") that focus on "basic skills" and at some point lost track of the original purpose of public education.

The school of today, therefore, resulted in a complex program that lacks the clarity of vision of its founders. But even if it had not, the fact is that the 150-year-old model based on the needs (and pedagogical knowledge) of an industrial revolution era society are completely out of touch with the new realities of the twenty-first century. Moreover, although the research in cognitive sciences, psychology, and education has advanced by leaps and bounds in the past century and presents with a solid empirical basis regarding what are the best and most efficient ways to educate children, the educational and political establishments have largely ignored the science or have applied it only sporadically (Aronson & Osherow, 1980; Kohn, 1999; McCombs & Whisler, 1997). What are the most pressing problems of today's schools that are holding back all of our children, but particularly minority children who come from underprivileged backgrounds to begin with?

Testing and Grading

There is plenty of evidence suggesting that the standardized testing we have come to rely so much on is not only problematic and inaccurate, but outright harmful. First, even if we were to agree with the premise that these tests are a valid and reliable measure of the effectiveness of learning in our schools, as more states and institutions create more of these tests (that our children are required to take now every year from grades three to eight), less emphasis is being placed on safeguarding them against cultural bias, that is a real issue in the testing of minorities, but tends to be largely dismissed (Bernal, 2000; Bernal & Valencia, 2000; Fassold, 2000; Valencia & Salinas, 2000; Valencia, Villareal, & Salinas, 2002).

However, that is only the tip of the iceberg. Tests, even if reliable, valid, and unbiased, are problematic because they tend to measure a very limited range of abilities that have no relationship with some of the most important qualities of a successful student (Ayers, 1993; Kohn, 1999), as for example, critical thinking, creativity, ingenuity, initiative, teamwork, leadership, democracy, diversity, or curiosity. Some studies have actually found that students who do better on tests tend to have more superficial engagement of learning (Meece, Blumenfeld, & Hoyle, 1988), have less intrinsic motivation (Deci, Vallerand, Pelletier, & Ryan, 1991), and are less self-regulated (Zimmerman, 1994). As Delisle (1997) points out, these tests penalize the most gifted and creative students:

There are countless cases of magnificent student writers whose work was labeled as "not proficient" because it did not follow the step-by-step sequence of what the test scorers (many of whom are not educators, by the way) think good expository writing should look like. And, with many of the multiple-choice questions having several "correct" options in the eyes of creative thinkers, scores get depressed for children who see possibilities that are only visible to those with open minds. (p. 42)

Finally, tests are dangerous because they lead teachers to "teach to the test," or in other words, the emphasis is on one-time high performance and concrete, well-defined problems with definite correct/incorrect solutions, instead of long-term mastery and analytical skills needed to solve ill-defined, complex situations in which solutions are not African American and White, correct or incorrect (which happens to be the case in real life). Once students, and then teachers and schools, are evaluated and rewarded on the basis of standardized test performance, the whole school curriculum changes to achieve the highest overall scores possible (Kohn, 1999). Education turns from an experience of growth and openmindedness into one of endless drills and repetition that can achieve the best possible test scores, but not the best learning.

Extrinsic Motivation

When children are 4–5 years old, they function as little learning sponges: they are fascinated by the discovery, and learning in itself serves as a reward, a process that we call "intrinsic motivation." However, by the time they reach elementary school, children quickly learn that learning in itself is not the point, but that an external reward (such as a grade, but sometimes candy, toys, privileges, and even gifts from their parents) is the ultimate goal, and learning is just a means to acquire the goodies, in other words, "extrinsic motivation." Intrinsically motivated students not only perform better academically, even when measured by standardized testing (Gottfried, 1985, 1990; Pintrich & DeGroot, 1990; Zsolnai, 2002), but also, have lower dropout rates (Vallerand & Bissonnette, 1992; Vallerand, Fortier, & Guay, 1997), higher level conceptual thinking (Benware & Deci, 1984; Grolnik & Ryan, 1987), more positive emotions and academic satisfaction (Vallerand, Blais, Briere, & Pelletier, 1989, as reported in Deci et al., 1991; Zsolnai, 2002), lower anxiety and better coping skills (Gottfried, 1990), and higher self-esteem (see, for example, Deci, Schwartz, Sheinman, & Ryan, 1981; Kasser & Ryan, 2001; Makri-Botsari, 2001). The paradox is that in spite of a growing body of research that supports the suggestion that intrinsically motivated learning is vastly superior to the extrinsic type, not only are the techniques and methodologies used in school not geared toward enhancing intrinsic motivation, but, in fact, the use of grades and other incentives and the increased reliance on standardized testing greatly undermines intrinsic motivation (for example, Butler, 1988; Deci, Koestner, & Ryan, 1999, 2001; Kohn, 1993).

Passive Learning

The famous Irish poet William Yeats once said, "Education is not the filling of a pail but the lighting of a fire." He had no idea how far ahead of his time he was in terms of the psychology of learning. Until the 1960s, psychologists believed that learning was a process in which a passive learner associated behaviors and consequences by way of the actions of an active "teacher." Since then, however, it has become increasingly clear that learning is not a passive process of absorbing information, but, rather, a very dynamic one in which the learner actively organizes, structures, and attaches meaning to the information he or she receives. Research in the past decade has strongly supported the idea that knowledge is *constructed*, rather than absorbed, by the learner as we attempt to make sense of new information (see, for example, Fosnot, 1996; Fosnot & Dolk, 2001; Hiebert & Raphael, 1996; Mayer, 1996).

Furthermore, it has become increasingly apparent that this construction of knowledge occurs best when the learner is an active participant in the classroom that is supported or *scaffolded* by a teacher who functions as a facilitator (see, for example, Heller & Hungate, 1984; Pugh, 2002). This involves being a part in the decision process regarding setting their learning goals, choosing the content, and deciding on the evaluation methods and criteria (see, for example, Huba & Freed, 2000; Kohn, 1999; McCombs & Whisler, 1997). It also involves the use of cooperative and collaborative learning methods, such as reciprocal teaching (see, for example, Hacker & Tenent, 2002; King & Johnson, 1999), cooperative learning (see, for example, Gillies, 2002, 2003; Johnson & Johnson, 1990; Johnson, Johnson, & Taylor, 1993; Slavin & Cooper, 1999) and peer tutoring (see, for example, Cardona, 2002; Hooper & Walker, 2002; Stephenson & Warwick, 2001).

However, despite the overwhelming body of evidence supporting a more active, participatory type of learning as more meaningful and effective, we continue to support a teacher-centered and curriculum-centered model of education in which we expect all students in the class to learn the same material, at the same time.

Disparity in Educational Resources— De Facto Segregation

One of the cornerstones of the civil rights movement during the 1960s was the issue of school desegregation. Even for those of us who are not old enough to remember the story of the "Little Rock 9" at the Central High School in Little Rock, Arkansas; James Meredith's valiant attempt to integrate the University of Mississippi in 1962; and the image of Governor George Wallace standing at the door of the University of Alabama had a tremendous impact on the American psyche. It is precisely in that context that perhaps the biggest failure of our current public education establishment has been to end a state of de facto segregation in our schools. The facts are, that at the beginning of the twenty-first century, almost fifty years after the landmark *Brown v. Board of Education* Supreme Court case ended school segregation in 1954, schools have reverted to a state of segregation where urban schools have become largely minority while suburban and rural schools are mostly White (see, for example, Mintrom, 1993). Moreover, even as our schools remain racially divided, the growth of the suburbs, the pattern of real estate property values, and a funding scheme that closely relates these values with school funding, have created large differences in funding of urban/minority school districts versus their suburban counterparts (Gorman, 1999; Mintrom, 1993; Symonds, 2002). In fact, a recent study by the The Civil Rights Project at Harvard University (Frankenberg, Lee, & Orfield, 2003) found a steady pattern of resegregation for the past twelve years. These inequalities in terms of money and resources have a clear impact on student achievement. For example, Roscigno and Ainsworth-Darnell (1999) carried out a study which found that the gap in African American–White achievement, although related to the family's socioeconomic and education background, is largely explained by factors related to school finances such as educational return and classroom level. Also, Symonds (2002) relates school funding inequalities to minority achievement, as she explains that "spending discrepancies are one reason that, by the eighth grade, poor students are three years behind middle-class children in reading and math" (p. 124) and concludes that without comprehensive reform of the school-funding system, school achievement will depend on the location of the school just as much as on the ability and effort of the students.

It Is Based on Western/European Values

It is, of course, not the fault of Horace Mann and the other founders of the "Common School" that they based their educational philosophy on the Western, European ideas of modernization and industrialization that were *en vogue* at the time. After all, that is not only what they were familiar with, but also what fitted into their conception of the modern American society. However, as the demographic composition of the American public school changed, due in part to changing immigration patterns, but also to school desegregation and integration of minorities into the school system, a change in the educational paradigm should have occurred. For the most part, it did not.

The methods and content of any educational program are a reflection of the values and philosophy of a culture. As students from different cultural backgrounds integrated into the school system, they faced the double struggle of performing up to par with their peers who were culturally matched with the school, adapting to a philosophy of knowledge, an "epistemological belief," that did not necessarily match that of their culture. The scientific literature supports the suggestion that different cultures have different patterns of "learning styles,"* and therefore, would receive a more effective and enriching education if the "teaching style" they are exposed to matches the learning style of the student. For example, White students of European descent tend to favor visual, written, and numerical language and individual learning, and to analyze problems by breaking them into smaller parts to understand their connections. In contrast, African American students tend to prefer a more oral, auditory language style, hands-on tactile concrete activities, work in groups, and a more holistic perspective that sees a problem as a whole (Brown & Cooper, 1981; Hale-Benson, 1986; Melear & Alcock, 1998; Sternberg, 1994). Native Americans put an even greater emphasis on auditory language as opposed to a written one, since they have a long tradition of oral history (Richardson, 1981) but prefer a nonverbal, visual, spatial, and kinesthetic orientation. They learn better in environments with lots of movement and activity, and based on concrete examples instead of abstractions (Cajete, 1999). Hispanic students also perform better with visual/spatial learning, but they prefer symbolic, abstract representations and metaphors rather than concrete, rational examples to help them understand difficult concepts (Griggs & Dunn, 1996; Picou, Gatlin-Watts, & Packer, 1998). Like African Americans, they are better at

---

*Of course, these patterns are not to be thought of as stereotypical generalizations. There is still more variance within any specific culture than there is between cultures when it comes to learning styles.

working in groups and at understanding the big picture rather than the smaller parts (Baruth & Manning, 1992).

On the other hand, Asian American children tend to be more self-disciplined, value authority, and take responsibility (Lee & Lodewijks, 1995). They also prefer traditional seating arrangements, individual learning methods, and having a figure of authority in the classroom (Griggs & Dunn, 1996).

It does not seem coincidental, therefore, that in our public school system, where a teacher-centered, rational style that emphasizes written work and individual performance, White and Asian American students tend to adapt better and perform best while Hispanic and African American students have a harder time. In fact, several authors (see, for example, Roth & Damico, 1999; Shade, 1997; Smith, 1998) have conducted studies and developed models supporting the contention that the traditional public school does not cater to the learning styles of African Americans and Hispanics, and only through systemic changes that support different learning styles can minority populations (and for that matter, any child that has a learning style that is different from the norm) be properly served by our educational system.

Affirmative Action as Prevention

As I have previously discussed, affirmative action turned into a corrective measure to compensate for existing inequalities in the system. The result is that even though it has helped close the gap between minorities and women and White males, when the correction is removed, as in the cases of Texas and California, the inequalities persist. Turning affirmative action from an after-the-fact correction to a preventive intervention program that eliminates the disparity at its root is a task that has to be initiated at the front end of the problem: the most basic levels of the education system in the United States. The assumption, therefore, is that as we move away from deficit thinking (Menchaca, 1997; Valencia, 1997) education is not only a possible (perhaps even the best) solution to end racial disparities in our country, but, in fact, as I have discussed, a major cause of them.

The concept of turning education into a solution for racial inequalities is not new. For instance, Pratkanis, Turner, and Malos (2002) suggest a "helping model of affirmative action," which proposes that discriminatory barriers have to be removed proactively by challenging some of the core assumptions of an educational system adapted to a society that tolerates prejudice. Pratkanis and his colleagues further argue that real desegregation and school inequality can only be achieved through a more open, democratic model of schooling.

But to understand how our education system today actually fuels and promotes the ethnic disparity, it is necessary to understand something about the philosophy of education and the American vision of what education should be about.

Lamm (1976) divided educational models into three broad groups: Imitation, which is content centered; molding, which is society centered; and development, which is learner centered (see Table 5.1).

The goal of content-centered models is acculturation to content that is seen as intrinsically valuable because it reflects the norms and values of the culture. In a content-centered classroom, the predominant activity would be to pay attention to the instructor, who serves as an "expert" agent of knowledge; the student is seen as a member of a rather homogeneous group (and classes are arranged to be that way through tracking and other forms of ability grouping). In the framework of Bloom's (1956) taxonomy of educational objectives, these models could be very good at achieving the lower levels of learning (knowledge, comprehension, which pretty much involve rote memorization and paraphrasing) but could have a very hard time in promoting higher levels (application, analysis, synthesis and evaluation, which involve all complex cognitive learning functions such as problem solving, categorization, formulation, and creativity). This model is highly popular, for example, in Asian countries, where students are not expected to participate actively in the classroom and the lessons are rigid and predetermined by the curriculum.

On the other hand, society-centered models are more descriptive of most American classrooms. As I have discussed, the goal is not imitation, but, rather, socialization into values, roles, and behavior patterns accepted by the society. In this type of classroom, the student is considered a member of a heterogeneous group and the preferred classroom activity is interaction with the instructor in teacher-directed activities. Finally, motivation is achieved through external means (very often grades). These models are better at achieving higher level learning, especially application and analysis, but they still fail to promote the divergent (creative) thinking necessary to develop synthesis and evaluation skills. In addition, socialization is

Table 5.1
Educational Models

Communication	Imitation (Content Centered)	Molding (Society Centered)	Development (Learner Centered)
Goal of Education	Proficiency in areas seen as valuable by culture	Proficiency in areas determined by needs of society	Mastery in areas determined by the capacities, skills, and needs of the individual and then fitted into societal roles
Desired Achievements	To act according to given principles	To perform according to given models	To discover new principles—challenge
Motivation	Extrinsic leads to intrinsic	Extrinsic	Intrinsic
Communication	Unidirectional	Bidirectional	Multidirectional
Activities	Listening	Imitating	Exploring
Status of Student	Member of homogeneous group	Member of heterogeneous group	Individual
Status of Teacher	Cultural agent: serves the interest of society in general	Employee: serves the interest of his or her employer	Specialist: professional, serves the needs of the students
Evaluation	Quantitative-competitive	Qualitative- and quantitative-competitive	Qualitative-non competitive
Curriculum	Is rigid and has intrinsic value: the advancement of knowledge for the sake of knowledge	Flexible; utilitarian: specific behaviors to serve the needs of society	Determined by individual needs; means of developing learners capacities: the full development of individuals' cognitive, affective, and physical abilities

Source: Adapted from Lamm (1976).

problematic for students from diverse backgrounds, not only because it has as a goal to conform to social norms and standards, but because it dictates that the teaching techniques and methodologies, as well as the learning styles of the students, conform to those same norms. If the norms and standards of a different culture are different, an "objective" evaluation will find them lacking in this type of model (for example, distinctive cultural characteristics like oral tradition versus written history, or focus on past versus focus on present, will show as "low performance").

Finally, in sharp contrast, learner-centered models are much better at promoting the highest levels of thinking. They are popular today in active learning circles, but they are far from being widespread in the American higher education system. The goal of learner-cenetered models is to support the student in achieving the maximum possible level of personal growth and development. This means that the individual student is at the center of the classroom, with a high degree of choice regarding content and activities, and therefore the student's motivation is intrinsic. In a learner-centered classroom, the most common activities are self-directed and cooperative learning with guidance (scaffolding) from the instructor. Up until this point, however, these models have been considered highly impractical for several reasons: It is hard to cover as much material as in the other models (which are better at Bloom's lower levels), students tend to wander and they might lose focus, teachers have to work a lot harder with smaller groups to serve as facilitators, and quantitative, competitive evaluation is hard to accomplish.

Because of the increase in empirical support for constructivist, learner-centered models of learning, in 1990, the American Psychological Association appointed a special Presidential Task Force on Psychology in Education whose objective was twofold: (1) to determine ways in which the psychological knowledge base related to learning, motivation, and individual differences could contribute directly to improvements in the quality of student achievement, and (2) to provide guidance for the design of educational systems that would best support individual student learning and achievement (McCombs & Whisler, 1997). The result was an integrated set of principles that reflect the best practices, as supported by psychological and educational research, to improve education for all. "Taken as a whole [the learner-centered principles] provide an integrated perspective on factors influencing learning for all learners. Together, they are intended to be understood as an organized knowledge base that supports a learner-centered model" (McCombs & Whisler, 1997, p. 3). By definition, because learner-centered education focuses on the needs and expectations of the individual learner, it eliminates many of the biases, cultural and otherwise, of traditional, curriculum-centered education and should therefore be able to reduce the growing academic performance gap.

Furthermore, minorities in schools and classrooms with higher learner-centered orientations attain more positive outcomes when compared to minorities in traditional schools. First, it appears that their academic performance indicators are closer to those of their White peers. But in addition, they also seem to exhibit higher scores in nontraditional measures of school success, such as creativity, motivation to learn, self-regulation, cooperative skills, openness to diversity, and metacognitive skills.

Learner-Centered Principles

The learner-centered model and principles were first compiled in 1993 by the American Psychological Association Presidential Task Force, and then further developed by McCombs and Whisler (1997). The revised model includes fourteen principles clustered in four areas (see Table 5.2).

Since their publication, the principles have inspired a large number of studies and educational programs. These, in turn, have provided evidence suggesting that learner-centered schools are more effective than traditional education in promoting both traditional indicators of school performance such as achievement (Fasko & Grubb, 1997; Matthews & McLaughlin, 1994; Ovando & Alford, 1997; Perry; 1999) and graduation rates (Ancess, 1995), as well as other, less traditional indicators, like motivation (Daniels, Kalkman, & McCombs, 2001), student self-regulation (Salisbury-Glennon, Gorrell, Sanders, Boyd, & Kamen, 1999), self-efficacy and self-esteem (Ancess, 1995; Fasko & Grubb, 1997; Houle, 1992; Perry, 1999), creativity (Hamilton, 1999; Rallis, 1996; Schuh, 2001), and finally tolerance, diversity, and multiculturalism (Donohue, 2001; Houle, 1992; Rallis, 1996; Sewell, DuCette, & Shapiro, 1998; Thornton and McEntee, 1995; Udvari-Solner & Thousand, 1996).

Table 5.2
Learner-Centered Principles

Cognitive and Metacognitive Factors

1. *Nature of the learning process.* The learning of complex subject matter is most effective when it is an intentional process of constructing meaning from information and experience.
2. *Goals of the learning process.* The successful learner, over time and with support and instructional guidance, can create meaningful, coherent representations of knowledge.
3. *Construction of knowledge.* The successful learner can link new information with existing knowledge in meaningful ways.
4. *Strategic thinking.* The successful learner can create and use a repertoire of thinking and reasoning strategies to achieve complex learning goals.
5. *Thinking about thinking.* Higher order strategies for selecting and monitoring mental operations facilitate creative and critical thinking.
6. *Context of learning.* Learning is influenced by environmental factors, including culture, technology, and instructional practices.

Motivational and Affective Factors

7. *Motivational and emotional influences on learning.* What and how much is learned is influenced by the learner's motivation. Motivation to learn, in turn, is influenced by the individual's emotional state, beliefs, interests and goals, and habits of thinking.
8. *Intrinsic motivation to learn.* The learner's creativity, higher order thinking, and natural curiosity all contribute to motivation to learn. Intrinsic motivation is stimulated by tasks of optimal novelty and difficulty, relevant to personal interests, and provides for personal choice and control.
9. *Effects of motivation on effort.* Acquisition of complex knowledge and skills requires extended learner effort and guided practice. Without learners' motivation to learn, the willingness to exert this effort is unlikely without coercion.

Developmental and Social Factors

10. *Developmental influences on learning.* As individuals develop, there are different opportunities and constraints for learning. Learning is most effective when differential development within and across physical, intellectual, emotional, and social domains is taken into account.
11. *Social influences on learning.* Learning is influenced by social interactions, interpersonal relations, and communication with others.

(continued)

Table 5.2
Learner-Centered Principles (*continued*)

Individual Differences Factors

12. *Individual differences in learning*. Learners have different strategies, approaches, and capabilities for learning that are a function of prior experience and heredity.
13. *Learning and diversity*. Learning is most effective when differences in learners' linguistic, cultural, and social backgrounds are taken into account.
14. *Standards and assessment*. Setting appropriately high and challenging standards and assessing the learner as well as the learning progress—including diagnostic, process, and outcome assessment—are integral parts of the learning process.

Source: Adapted from American Psychological Association (1997).

One example of a study supporting increased achievement, is one performed by Matthews and McLaughlin (1995). In their study, a group of twelfth graders who participated in a biology course were either assigned to a traditional lecture class or to a learner-centered lecture plus guided laboratory class. Scores on a posttest requiring higher level reasoning showed that the students in the learner-centered class scored significantly higher. Similarly, in a field study by Fasko and Grubb (1997), sixth to twelfth grade teachers and students from a rural school system rated themselves using a learner-centered teacher survey and were also rated by their students. Fasko and Grubb found that effective teachers demonstrated more implementation of learner-centered principles, and that the level of implementation predicted student achievement.

Regarding some of the less traditional indicators of school success, a number of studies showed very interesting results. For example, in one study, Salisbury-Glennon, Gorrell, Sanders, Boyd, and Kamen (1999) collected data on 114 sixth and seventh graders from an urban middle-class school in two multiage classrooms that used a learner-centered approach. The researchers found that these students exhibited a number of characteristics that are indicative of self-regulation, such as an orientation toward "developing new skills, the intrinsic value of learning, developing their understanding, and improvement" (p. x).

In another study, Daniels, Kalkman, and McCombs (2001) interviewed children grades K to 2, and found that the children's motivation for learning and interest in schoolwork was significantly higher in learner-centered classrooms than in more traditional classrooms.

Of special relevance to minority students and students from other diverse backgrounds is that one of the most compelling areas in which learner-centered models appear to make an impact is in the area of tolerance, diversity, and multiculturalism. This is especially important in an era in which there is renewed focus on bullying and stereotyping in the schools after Columbine and other school violence incidents. For instance, Donohue (2001) examined whether a more learner-centered environment in the classroom leads to lower rates of rejection by peers. She collected data from twenty-eight kindergarten and first grade teachers. Her analysis revealed that learner-centered methodologies are linked to lower levels of peer rejection.

A Paradigm Shift

In conclusion, the evidence suggests that learner-centered models actually develop qualities in students that are most valuable in a free society that is moving away from an industrial model and into an "information age" one: initiative, responsibility, creativity, intrinsic motivation, analytic skills, cooperation, and so on. Furthermore, in theory, because learner-centered models are focused on the individual student as opposed to the curriculum, each student, regardless of their gender or ethnicity, can perform to the best of their abilities without sacrificing their own cultural patterns and personal learning styles. Although there is still a lot of research needed to clearly identify the effects of learner-centered models on minority students, there are some studies that support this idea.

For example, McCombs (2001) reviews a number of studies about the effects of learner-centered approaches in predominantly minority urban schools. The studies she reviewed collected data from more than five thousand students grades K to 8. Although she reports a disturbing pattern of decreased learner-centeredness in these schools as students progress to the higher grades, she also found a strong relationship among the learner-centered orientation and achievement, student motivation, increased attendance, reduced disruptive behaviors, positive adult–youth relationships, and, overall, a better school climate and a culture of caring. Even the teachers from urban schools, who tend to be more prone to stress and high attrition rates, reported to have lower levels of stress and higher job satisfaction in learner-centered environments (Krudwig, 2000).

Elliot Aronson (2002), the renowned social psychologist better know for developing the "jigsaw classroom methodology," also argues about the benefits of learner-centered environments, such as the one the jigsaw classroom provides, for students form diverse backgrounds and ethnic groups. In the jigsaw classroom, students are divided into small groups. Each individual student is responsible for a project, which he or she must report back to the small group. These projects are then assembled (like a jigsaw) to form a larger picture of the topic being studied. Aronson has used and researched this technique for over thirty years, and reports that it not only improves the academic performance and motivation of minorities, but reduces racial conflict and improves empathy and socialization among students of all backgrounds.

Another researcher, Arthur Pearl (1997) proposes that democratic education, the philosophy first developed by John Dewey which fits the learner-centered model, can be used as an alternative to traditional models which, according to Pearl, promote deficit thinking (Valencia, 1997).

Pearl believes that current models of educational practice designed to correct the gap between minorities and nonminorities (which he categorizes as compensatory education and effective education) are insufficient because they address the problem in a superficial manner that is focused on performance. Furthermore, he believes that the current models perpetuate the problem because their authoritarian nature and the conception that schooling is actually the problem to be solved place the blame on the school itself without reexamining society as a whole. Rather, Pearl suggests, democratic education becomes an alternative because it not only provides students with an equal, high-quality education, but also makes them active participants in the educational process, and provides them with the tools and the information they need to confront the social problems that he sees as the real cause for educational failure of minorities. He believes that in order to be successful, democratic education has to have four components: (1) knowledge—the information and tools the student needs and is active in choosing to make a difference in the world; (2) participation—all students are active participants in the educational process; (3) rights—to dignity, to equality, and to information; and (4) equal encouragement—all students are equally important and equally capable of excelling.

Although the concept of a learner-centered revolution is, in principle, very attractive and persuasive, in fact more research is still needed in order to develop a large-scale learner-centered program that could help eliminate the gap between minorities and Whites. This is a monumental task since our massive public education system is rooted as much on inertia as it is on the principles of a socializing education. However, if we were to ever change our schools to a learner-centered model, what would our classroom look like?

The first thing that strikes you from a learner-centered classroom is the lack of structure. Chairs and tables are not neatly organized in rows. Students, who many times are from different ages, are not all sitting down but moving and walking. Teachers are not in front of a classroom delivering the lesson, but talking to the students individually, kneeling, and going around time and time again. People that are used to a traditional classroom might get the impression that this is highly unstructured. As a matter of fact, it is not. Each student is working on a specific project, knows what he or she is supposed to do, and is keenly aware of the standards expected from them in their work. The learner-centered classroom might not have the orderliness of an assembly-line-like operation, but if you are familiar with the high-tech industry, they actually resemble quite closely a busy department in a company like Microsoft, Oracle, or IBM: People working in teams or individually, being highly creative and productive, in a process of discovery and exchange of ideas that breeds new knowledge. Another example of apparent chaos is the Stock Exchange, in which, at first glance, people appear to be screaming and moving aimlessly around the floor of the exchange. Yet, in reality, it is a very structured and efficient process in which each member has a specific role that they are expected to fulfill flawlessly. Despite of the apparent disarray, no one would accuse these organizations of being unstructured or inefficient because their workers are not all sitting down working silently on the same project. Yet, many people do not hesitate to level this charge to learner-centered classrooms. This reflects a misconception of what a learner-centered environment really is. Table 5.3 lists the characteristics of a learner-centered classroom.

Table 5.3
Characteristics of the Learner-Centered Classroom

In learner-centered classrooms, the students

- Choose their own project
- Work at their own individual pace
- Show excitement about learning new things
- Work with students of different ages, cultures and abilities
- Demonstrate their knowledge in unique ways
- Are actively engaged and participating in individual and group learning activities
- Go beyond minimal assignments

In learner-centered classrooms, the teacher

- Makes it clear that he/she has high expectations for all students
- Listens to and respects each student's point of view
- Encourages and facilitates student's participation and shared decision making
- Provides structure without being overly directive
- Encourages students to think for themselves
- Emphasizes student enjoyment of activities
- Helps students refine their strategies for constructing meaning and organizing content

In learner-centered classrooms, the instructional strategies and methods

- Use time in variable and flexible ways to match student needs
- Include learning activities that are personally relevant to students
- Give students increasing responsibility for the learning process
- Provide questions and tasks that stimulate students' thinking beyond rote memorizing
- Help students refine their understanding by using critical thinking skills
- Support students in developing and using effective learning strategies
- Include peer learning and peer teaching as part of the instructional method

In learner-centered classrooms, the curriculum

- Features tasks that stimulate students' varied interests
- Organizes content and activities around themes that are meaningful to students
- Has explicit built-in opportunities for all students to engage their higher-order thinking and self-regulated learning skills
- Includes activities that help students understand and develop their own perspectives
- Allows learning activities that are global, interdisciplinary, and integrated
- Encourages challenging learning activities, even if students have difficulty
- Features activities that encourage students to work collaboratively with other students

(continued)

Table 5.3
Characteristics of the Learner-Centered Classroom (*continued*)

In learner-centered classrooms, the assessment system
- Assesses different students differently
- Includes student input in design and revision
- Monitors progress continually in order to provide feedback on individual growth and progress
- Provides appropriate opportunities for student choice of types of products for demonstrating achievement of educational standards
- Promotes student's reflection on their growth as learners through opportunities for self-assessment
- Allows diversity of competencies to be demonstrated in a variety of ways

Source: McCombs & Whisler, 1997, p. 65–66

However, as in any other paradigm shift in history, there are a number of major obstacles to overcome in order to accomplish this transition. The first, and most difficult, challenge in implementing this model is to develop a change in the American culture of schooling. In recent years, and in spite of the research and the support of academia, we have not only not seen our schools getting closer to learner-centered models, but, in fact, they have been moving further away as initiatives such as "no child left behind" and movements like "back to basics" and phonics instruction emphasize a traditional model of teaching and increase the role of standardized testing and rote memorization of facts. These initiatives and movements will be hard to overcome because they are politically popular, even though (or perhaps because of) they simplify education to the extreme, basically erasing individual differences in the classroom.

Another big obstacle is our teaching culture. The role of the traditional teacher will change dramatically in a new learner-centered classroom. In a more individual/collaborative learning setting, instead of being a leader, the teacher becomes a guide and a facilitator. Today's teachers are not trained for those roles, and educational development models, teacher's unions, and teacher certification programs are reputedly resistant to change.

Last, there are important issues regarding funding. Learner-centered education does require smaller student–teacher ratios and investments in technology. Although it is widely accepted that a learner-centered classroom is more expensive to run than a traditional one, there are no specific reports dealing with this issue, and evaluations of schools that have adopted learner-centered models do not relate to budgetary issues as one of their main concerns (see, for example, Burrello, Lashley, & Beatty, 2001; Canedo & Woodard, 2000; Davis, Pool, & Mits-Cash, 2000; Hawley, 2002; Page, 2001), which indicates that whatever the per-pupil expenditures in these programs, they were not significantly higher than traditional ones, since otherwise they would have certainly come up as a major issue. Furthermore, Levin (1994) even argues that learner-centered schools are, after all, more productive, and even if slightly more expensive, from an economical point of view, the fact that they are more productive and efficient makes them more cost-effective.

Conclusion

A paradigm shift in the model of schooling in America is a project of gargantuan proportions that would entail changing social, political, and cultural views on education. It is a project that would need to be started as a grassroots movement, educating parents and teachers about the benefits of learner-centered education not only in terms of the ethnic and racial inequalities that exist in America, but about the overall benefit that these models have on helping children grow, develop, and become critical thinkers, or as Shaull (1970) said, education becomes "the means by which men and women deal critically and creatively with reality and discover how to participate in the transformation of their world" (p. 4). However, even with grassroots support, big changes can only happen if a new generation of leaders, both political and social, who are visionary and motivated, is willing to put forward a bold agenda and confront all the challenges that would emerge to effect this radical change in American education.

Epilogue

There are a number of messages that we can garner from this book. The first is that affirmative action was an emergency stopgap measure that was required to solve a very serious, immediate problem that could not wait any longer to be addressed. As such, like most other temporary corrective measures, it was imperfect: The guidelines were vague, its definition unclear, based on a misguided understanding of merit, and was the result of a more ephemeral presidential executive order instead of a more concrete legislative bill. That, however, was secondary because just like a bucket placed under the ceiling to collect water dripping from above, affirmative action was not intended nor designed to solve the underlying problems of inequality in American society, just to provide a needed "correction" that would balance or compensate for the inequalities which, to this date, exist in our society.

The second point is that stereotypes and prejudice in American society, contrary to what many believe, have not disappeared from American society. Prejudice has been transformed from its crass and overt form of the 1950s to a more subtle and indirect form, but is still prevalent. Furthermore, stereotypes, but sometimes even prejudice and racism, are still a powerful force in shaping social and political thinking at the beginning of the new millennium. Real equality and a color-blind society are not possible under these circumstances.

The third message that we can get from this book, therefore, is that a long-term program is needed to solve the problem of inequality, not just to compensate for it. Affirmative action was originally needed, and is still needed today, because of the disparities (social, economical, political, and educational) that we have in America. If we solve this fundamental problem, if, as Dr. Martin Luther King dreamed, we have a society in which all people are equal, affirmative action would become obsolete of its own weight and we would not have the need to debate "ending" it, or "amending" it, or anything else. We should look at a new kind of affirmative action as intervention, as a long-term program to attack the root causes of inequality and prejudice. Affirmative action should not be about stopping the drippings but about fixing the ceiling, because once the ceiling is fixed, the bucket becomes unnecessary.

The final message this book conveys is that the road to end ethnic and gender disparity in America has to start with education reform. Only when we are ready to abandon an antiquated educational model designed to serve an emerging industrial society, and based on the values of the dominant White class of the time, will education begin to serve all its students equally. Only when each child is treated as an individual learner, and the classroom and curriculum is based on their unique needs, will truly "no child be left behind." Only when funding and resources meet the needs of each school in America, and we end the inequalities with schools, the first institution to serve our young future citizens, can we hope that inequality will disappear from the rest of society.

The road to redemption, however, is long and hard. A program as ambitious as one like this would take at least a generation to complete, and would fight immense opposition from interests that are set to lose if we change the current system. Usually, that is a lot more and a lot longer than our political class is able to swallow. Therefore, to effect this change, we cannot do it by electing a party or a president. We have to understand and accept this idea at a more cultural and social level. In other words, we have to have the courage to change ourselves if we really want to change the world.

References

Works Cited

Adorno, T., Frenkel-Brunswick, E., Levinson, D., & Sanford, R. (1950). *The authoritarian personality*. New York: Harper.

Agresti, A., & Finlay B. (1997). *Statistical methods for the social sciences* (3rd ed.). New York: Prentice-Hall.

Alexander, K. L., Entwisle, D. R., & Bedinger, S. D. (1994). When expectations work: Race and socioeconomic differences in school performance. *Social Psychology Quarterly, 57*(4), 283–299.

Allport, G. W. (1954). *The nature of prejudice*. Reading, MA: Addison-Wesley.

American Psychological Association. (1997). *Learner-centered psychological principles: A framework for school redesign and reform*. Available: http://www.apa.org/ed/lcp.html

Anastasi, A., & Urbina, S. (1997). *Psychological testing*. Upper Saddle River, NJ: Prentice-Hall.

Ancess, J. (1995). *An inquiry high school: Learner-centered accountability at the urban academy*. New York: Teachers College Press. (ERIC Document Reproduction Service No. ED 385 648)

Aronson, E. (2002). Building empathy, compassion, and achievement in the jigsaw classroom. In J. Aronson (Ed.), *Improving academic achievement: Impact of psychological factors on education* (pp. 209–225). San Diego, CA: Academic Press.

Aronson, E., & Osherow, N. (1980). Cooperation, prosocial behavior, and academic performance: Experiments in the desegregated classroom. *Applied Social Psychology Annual, 1*, 163–196.

Aronson, J. (2002). Stereotype threat: Contending and coping with unnerving expectations. In J. Aronson (Ed.), *Improving academic achievement: Impact of psychological factors on education* (pp. 279–301). San Diego, CA: Academic Press.

Aronson, J., Lustina, M. J., Good, C., Keough, K., Steele, C. M., & Brown, J. (1999). When White men can't do math: Necessary and sufficient factors in stereotype threat. *Journal of Experimental Social Psychology, 35*(1), 29–46.

Aronson, J., Steele, C. M., Salinas, M. F., & Lustina, M. J. (1999). The effect of stereotype threat on the standardized test performance of college students. In E. Aronson (Ed.), *Readings about the social animal* (8th ed., pp. 415–430). New York: Worth.

Artiles, A. J., & Trent, S. C. (1994). Overrepresentation of minority students in special education: A continuing debate. *Journal of Special Education, 27*(4), 410–437.

Ashmore R., & Del Boca, F. (1981). Conceptual approaches to stereotypes and stereotyping. In D. Hamilton (Ed.), *Cognitive processes in stereotyping and intergroup behavior* (pp. 1–36). Hillsdale, NJ: Erlbaum.

Ayers. H. (1993). *Assessing individual needs: A practical approach*. London: D. Fulton

Bandura, A. (1986). *Social foundations of thought and action: A social cognitive theory*. Rockville, MD: National Institute of Mental Health.

Barnett, W. S. (1998). Long-term cognitive and academic effects of early childhood education of children in poverty. *Preventive Medicine: An International Journal Devoted to Practice & Theory, 27*(2), 204–207.

Baruth, L. G., & Manning, M. L. (1992). Understanding and counseling Hispanic American children. *Elementary School Guidance & Counseling, 27*(2), 113–122.

Basco, W. T., Jr., Gilbert, G. E., Chessman, A. W., & Blue, A. V. (2000). The ability of a medical school admission process to predict clinical performance and patients' satisfaction. *Academic Medicine, 75*(7), 743–747.

Beckum, L. C. (1983). Testing and the minority child. *New Directions for Testing & Measurement, 19*, 39–47.

Belliveau, M. A. (1996). The paradoxical influence of policy exposure on affirmative action attitudes. [Special issue]. *Journal of Social Issues, 52*(4), 99–104.

Bento, R. F. (1997). When good intentions are not enough: Unintentional subtle discrimination against Latinas in the workplace. In N. V. Benokraitis (Ed.), *Subtle sexism: Current practice and prospects for change* (pp. 95–116). Thousand Oaks, CA: Sage.

Benware, C. A., & Deci, E. L. (1984). Quality of learning with an active versus passive motivational set. *American Educational Research Journal, 21*(4), 755–765.

Bernal, E. M. (2000). Psychometric inadequacies of the TAAS. *Hispanic Journal of Behavioral Sciences, 22,* 481–507.

Bernal, E. M., & Valencia, R. R. (2000). The TAAS case: A recapitulation and beyond. *Hispanic Journal of Behavioral Sciences, 22*(4), 540–556.

Blacks still angry over white woman who claimed black man kidnapped her two boys. (1994, November 28). *Jet,* p. 16.

Bloom, B. S. (Ed.). (1956). *Taxonomy of educational objectives: The classification of educational goals,* Handbook I, *Cognitive domain.* New York: Longmans, Green.

Bobo, L., & Kluegel, J. R. (1993). Opposition to race-targeting: Self-interest, stratification ideology, or racial attitudes? *American Sociological Review, 58*(4), 443–464.

Bobocel, D. R., Davey, L. M., Son Hing, L. S., & Zanna, M. P. (2001). The concern for justice and reactions to affirmative action: Cause or rationalization? In R. Cropanzano (Ed.), *Justice in the workplace: From theory to practice* (Vol. 2, pp. 121–143). Mahwah, NJ: Erlbaum.

Bornstein, R. F. (1993). Mere exposure effects with out-group stimuli. In D. M. Mackie & D. L. Hamilton (Eds.), *Affect, cognition, and stereotyping: Interactive processes in group perception* (pp. 195–211). San Diego, CA: Academic Press.

Brown, J. F., & Cooper, R. M. (1981). *Learning styles inventory for Macintosh hyperCard.* Freeport, NY: Educational Activities.

Brown, R. P., Charnsangavej, T., Keough, K. A., Newman, M. L., & Rentfrow, P. J. (2000). Putting the "affirm" into affirmative action: Preferential selection and academic performance. *Journal of Personality & Social Psychology, 79*(5), 736–747.

Brugnoli, G. A., Campion, J. E., & Basen, J. A. (1979). Racial bias in the use of work samples for personnel selection. *Journal of Applied Psychology, 64*(2), 119–123.

Brutus, S., & Ryan, A. M. (1998). A new perspective on preferential treatment: The role of ambiguity and self-efficacy. *Journal of Business & Psychology, 13*(2), 157–178.

Bureau of Census. (2002). *Statistical abstract of the U.S.: 2000.* Washington, DC: U.S. Government Printing Office.

Burrello, L. C., Lashley, C., & Beatty, E. E. (2001). Educating all students together: How school leaders create unified systems. Thousand Oaks, CA: Corwin Press. (ERIC Document Reproduction Service No. ED 448 539)

Butler, R. (1988). Enhancing and undermining intrinsic motivation: The effects of task-involving and ego-involving evaluation of interest and performance. *British Journal of Educational Psychology, 58*(1), 1–14.

Cahn, S. M. (Ed.). (1995). *The affirmative action debate.* New York: Routledge.

Cajete, G. A. (1999). *The Native American learner and bicultural science education.* (Report No. RC021804). Albuquerque, NM: Rural Education and Small Schools. (ERIC Document Reproduction Service No. ED 427 908)

California Secretary of State. (1996). *Prohibition against discrimination or preferential treatment by state and other public entities. Initiative constitutional amendment.* Retrieved January 20, 2003. Available: http://vote96.ss.ca.gov/BP/209.htm

Campbell, D. T. (1965). Ethnocentric and other altruistic motives. In D. Levine (Ed.), *Symposium on motivation* (pp. 283–311). Lincoln: University of Nebraska Press.

Canedo, M., & Woodard, C. (2000). Learner-centered sites. *Childhood Education, 76*(5), 289–291.

Cardona, C. (2002). Adapting instruction to address individual and group educational needs in math. *Journal of Research in Special Educational Needs, 2*(1), 1–17.

Carmines, E. G., & Layman, G. C. (1998). When prejudice matters: The impact of racial stereotypes on the racial policy preferences of Democrats and Republicans. In J. Hurwitz and M. Peffley (Eds.), *Perception and prejudice: Race and politics in the United States* (pp. 100–134). New Haven, CT: Yale University Press.

Carter, S. L. (1993). Affirmative action harms Black professionals. In A. E. Sadler (Ed.), *Affirmative action* (pp. 48–65). San Diego, CA: Greenhaven.

Cascio, W. F., Outtz, J., & Zedeck, S. (1995). Statistical implications of six methods of test score use in personnel selection. *Human Performance, 8*(3), 133–164.

Center for Survey Research and Analysis. (2000, April). *A reaction to ballot-test questions on the policy of granting preferences in employment and admissions: A survey of faculty at Connecticut institutions of higher education.* Designed by the Connecticut Association of Scholars. Data collected by the University of Connecticut–Storrs.

Chacko, T. I. (1982). Women and equal employment opportunity: Some unintended effects. *Journal of Applied Psychology, 67*(1), 119–123.

Children Now Foundation. (2002). *Fallcolors: 2001–2002 prime time diversity report.* Available: http://www.childrennow.org

Coates, B. (1972). White adult behavior toward black and white children. *Child Development, 43*(1), 143–154.

Cohen, M. N. (1998). *Culture of intolerance: Chauvinism, class, and racism in the United States*. New Haven, CT: Yale University Press.

Cornwell, T. (1998, April 10). The *Times* higher education supplement. *The Los Angeles Times*, p. 8.

Crocker, J., & Major, B. (1989). Social stigma and self-esteem: The self-protective properties of stigma. *Psychological Review, 96*(4), 608–630.

Daniels, D. H., Kalkman, D. L., & McCombs, B. L. (2001). Young children's perspectives on learning and teacher practices in different classroom contexts: Implications for motivation. *Early Education and Development, 12*(2), 253–273.

Davis, D. R., Pool, J. E., & Mits-Cash, M. (2000). Issues in implementing a new teacher assessment system in a large urban school district: Results of a qualitative field study. *Journal of Personnel Evaluation in Education, 14*(4), 285–306.

Deci, E. L., Koestner, R., & Ryan, R. M. (1999). A meta-analytic review of experiments examining the effects of extrinsic rewards on intrinsic motivation. *Psychological Bulletin, 125*(6), 627–668.

Deci, E. L., Koestner, R., & Ryan, R. M. (2001). Extrinsic rewards and intrinsic motivation in education: Reconsidered once again. *Review of Educational Research, 71*(1), 1–27.

Deci, E. L., Schwartz, A. J., Sheinman, L., & Ryan, R. M. (1981). An instrument to assess adults' orientations toward control versus autonomy with children: Reflections on intrinsic motivation and perceived competence. *Journal of Educational Psychology, 73*(5), 642–650.

Deci, E. L., Vallerand, R. J., Pelletier, L. G., & Ryan, R. M. (1991). Motivation and education: The self-determination perspective. *Educational Psychologist, 26*(3–4), 325–346.

Delisle, J. R. (1997). How proficiency tests fall short. *Education Week, 16*(27), 41–43.

Devine, P. G. (1989). Stereotypes and prejudice: Their automatic and controlled components. *Journal of Personality & Social Psychology, 56*(1), 5–18.

Devine, P. G., & Elliot, A. J. (1995). Are racial stereotypes really fading? The Princeton Trilogy revisited. *Personality & Social Psychology Bulletin, 21*(11), 1139–1150.

Devlin, B., Fienberg, S. E., & Resnick, D. P. (2002). Intelligence and success: Is it all in the genes? In J. M. Fish (Ed.), *Race and intelligence: Separating science from myth* (pp. 355–368). Mahwah, NJ: Erlbaum.

Donohue, K. (2001). Classroom instructional practices and children's rejection by their peers. *Dissertation Abstracts International, 61*, 7A, p. 3839.

Douglass, J. A. (1998). Anatomy of conflict: the making and unmaking of affirmative action at the University of California. *American Behavioral Scientist, 41*(7), 938–959.

Doverspike, D., Taylor, M. A., & Winfred, A., Jr. (2000). *Affirmative action: A psychological perspective*. Huntington, NY: Nova Science.

Dovidio, J. F., & Gaertner, S. L. (1996). Affirmative action, unintentional racial biases, and intergroup relations. [Special issue]. *Journal of Social Issues, 52*(4), 51–75.

Dovidio, J. F., & Gaertner, S. L. (2000). Aversive racism and selection decisions: 1989 and 1999. *Psychological Science, 11*(4), 315–319.

Dovidio, J. F., Smith, J. K., Donnella, A. G., & Gaertner, S. L. (1997). Racial attitudes and the death penalty. *Journal of Applied Social Psychology, 27*(16), 1468–1487.

Duckitt, J. (1992). *The social psychology of prejudice*. New York: Praeger.

Duncan, B. L. (1976). Differential social perception and attribution of intergroup violence: Testing the lower limits of stereotyping of Blacks. *Journal of Personality & Social Psychology, 34*(4), 590–598.

Eagly, A. H. (1995). The science and politics of comparing women and men. *American Psychologist, 50*(3), 145–158.

Eastland, T. (1998, November 18). CCRI struggles on against critics and GOP cowardice. *The American Spectator, 29*(11), 65–68.

Edwards, J. C., Maldonado, F. G., Jr., & Calvin, J. A. (1999). The effects of differently weighting interview scores on the admission of underrepresented minority medical students. *Academic Medicine, 74*(1), 59–61.

Fairchild, H., & Gurin, P. (1978). Traditions in the social psychological analysis of race relations. *American Behavioral Scientist, 21*, 757–778.

Fasko, D., Jr., & Grubb, D. J. (1997, August). *Implications of the learner-centered battery for new teacher standards and teacher education reform in Kentucky*. Paper presented at the annual meeting of the American Psychological Association, Chicago, IL. (ERIC Document Reproduction Services No. ED 412 209)

Fassold, M. A. (2000). Disparate impact analyses of TAAS scores and school quality. *Hispanic Journal of Behavioral Sciences, 22*(4), 460–480.

Fazio, R. H., Jackson, J. R., & Dunton, B. C. (1995). Variability in automatic activation as an unobstrusive measure of racial attitudes: A bona fide pipeline? *Journal of Personality & Social Psychology, 69*(6), 1013–1027.

Feagin, J. R., & Sikes, M. P. (1994). *Living with racism: The black middle-class experience*. Boston: Beacon Press.

Federico, C. M., & Sidanius, J. (2002). Sophistication and the antecedents of Whites' racial policy attitudes: Racism, ideology, and affirmative action in America. *Public Opinion Quarterly, 66*(2), 145–176.

Fields, C. D. (1997). An equation for equality: Maryland's Prince George's County puts Equity 2000 to the test. *Black Issues in Higher Education, 13*(26), 24–30.

Fish, J. M. (Ed.) (2002). *Race and intelligence: Separating science from myth*. Mahwah, NJ: Erlbaum.

Fiske, S. (1993). Social cognition and social perception. *Annual Review of Psychology, 44*, 155–194.

Fiske, S. T. (2000). Interdependence and the reduction of prejudice. In S. Oskamp (Ed.), *Reducing prejudice and discrimination. The Claremont Symposium on Applied Social Psychology* (pp. 115–135). Mahwah, NJ: Erlbaum.

Fosnot, C. T. (1996). *Constructivism: Theory, perspectives, and practice.* New York: Teachers College Press.

Fosnot, C. T., & Dolk, M. L. (2001). *Young mathematicians at work: Constructing number sense, addition, and subtraction.* Portsmouth, NH: Heinemann.

Frankenberg, E., Lee, C., & Orfield, G. (2003). A multiracial society with segregated schools: Are we losing the dream? The Civil Rights Project at Harvard University. Cambridge, MA: Harvard University Press.

Frazer, R. A., & Wiersma, U. J. (2001). Prejudice versus discrimination in the employment interview: We may hire equally, but our memories harbor prejudice. *Human Relations, 54*(2), 173–191.

Gilbert, J. A., & Stead, B. A. (1999). Stigmatization revisited: Does diversity management make a difference in applicant success? *Group & Organization Management, 24*(2), 239–256.

Gilens, M. (1995). Racial-attitudes and opposition to welfare. *Journal of Politics, 57*(4), 994–1014.

Gillies, R. M. (2002). The residual effects of cooperative-learning experiences: A two-year follow-up. *Journal of Educational Research, 96*(1), 15–20.

Gillies, R. M. (2003). The behaviors, interactions, and perceptions of junior high school students during small-group learning. *Journal of Educational Psychology, 95*(1), 137–147.

Goldberg, H. (1994, March 3). Nation & world: Prejudice cuts across the board, poll finds. *Detroit Free Press*, p. A5.

Gorman, S. (1999). The education challenge. *National Journal, 31*(33), p. 2364.

Gose, B., & Selingo, J. (2001, October 26). The SAT's greatest test. *Chronicle of Higher Education*. Available: http://www.chronicle.com

Gottfried, A. E. (1985). Academic intrinsic motivation in elementary and junior high school students. *Journal of Educational Psychology, 77*(6), 631–645.

Gottfried, A. E. (1990). Academic intrinsic motivation in young elementary school children. *Journal of Educational Psychology, 82*(3), 525–538.

Graves, L. M., & Powell, G. N. (1994). Effects of sex-based preferential selection and discrimination on job attitudes. *Human Relations, 47*(2), 133–157.

Greenberger, M. D. (1995). Women need affirmative action. In A. E. Sadler (Ed.), *Affirmative action* (pp. 14–21). San Diego, CA: Greenhaven.

Griggs, S., & Dunn, R. (1996). *Hispanic-American students and learning style.* (Report No. EDD00036). Washington, DC: Office of Educational Research and Improvement. (ERIC Document Reproduction Service No. ED 393 607)

Grolnick, W. S., & Ryan, R. M. (1987). Autonomy in children's learning: An experimental and individual difference investigation. *Journal of Personality & Social Psychology, 52*(5), 890–898.

Hacker, D. J., & Tenent, A. (2002). Implementing reciprocal teaching in the classroom: Overcoming obstacles and making modifications. *Journal of Educational Psychology, 94*(4), 699–718.

Hale-Benson, J. E. (1986). *Black children: Their roots, culture, and learning styles.* Baltimore: John Hopkins University Press.

Hamilton, P. (1999). Reinventing the real. A training handbook for creativity and innovation with a contextual essay: Between two worlds. *Dissertation Abstracts International, 60,* 6B, p. 2972.

Hamm, N. H., Baum, M. R., & Nikels, K. W. (1975). Effects of race and exposure on judgments of interpersonal favorability. *Journal of Experimental Social Psychology, 11*(1), 14–24.

Haney, C., Banks, C., & Zimbardo, P. (1973). Interpersonal dynamics in a simulated prison. *International Journal of Criminology & Penology, 1*(1), 69–97.

Harding, J., Kutner, B., Proshansky, H., & Chein, I. (1954). Prejudice and ethnic relations. In G. Lindzey (Ed.), *Handbook of social psychology* (Vol. 2) (pp. 1021–1061). Cambridge, MA: Addison-Wesley.

Harding, J., Proshansky, H., Kutner, B., & Chein, I. (1969). Prejudice and ethnic relations. In G. Lindzey and E. Aronson (Eds.), *The handbook of social psychology* (Vol. 5) (pp. 1–76). Reading, MA: Addison-Wesley.

Harris, L. (1994). Changing trends in American politics: What in the world is going on in this nation? *Vital Speeches of the Day, 60*(21), 663–666.

Harris, L. (1995, April). *A survey of the attitudes of a cross-section of American women and men and a cross-section of voters in California on affirmative action, abortion, and other key issues affecting women and minorities.* 1995 Women's Equality Poll. Design and analysis by Louis Harris. Conducted by Peter Harris Research Group, New York.

Hartigan, J. A., & Wigdor, A. K. (1989). *Fairness in employment testing: Validity generalization, minority issues, and the General Aptitude Test Battery.* Washington, DC: National Academy Press.

Hawley, Willis D. (2002). The keys to effective schools: Educational reform as continuous improvement. Thousand Oaks, CA: Corwin Press. (ERIC Document Reproduction Service No. ED 461 940)

Heilman, M. E., & Alcott, V. B. (2001). What I think you think of me: Women's reactions to being viewed as beneficiaries of preferential selection. *Journal of Applied Psychology, 86*(4), 574–582.

Heilman, M. E., Battle, W. S., Keller, C. E., & Lee, R. A. (1998). Type of affirmative action policy: A determinant of reactions to sex-based preferential selection? *Journal of Applied Psychology, 83*(2), 190–205.

Heilman, M. E., Block, C. J., & Lucas, J. A. (1992). Presumed incompetent? Stigmatization and affirmative action efforts. *Journal of Applied Psychology, 77*(4), 536–544.

Heilman, M. E., McCullough, W. F., & Gilbert, D. (1996). The other side of affirmative action: Reactions of nonbeneficiaries to sex-based preferential selection. *Journal of Applied Psychology, 81*(4), 346–357.

Heilman, M. E., Simon, M. C., & Repper, D. P. (1987). Intentionally favored, unintentionally harmed? Impact of sex-based preferential selection on self-perceptions and self-evaluations. *Journal of Applied Psychology, 72*(1), 62–68.

Heller, J. I., & Hungate, H. N. (1984, April). *Theory-based instruction in description of mechanics problems.* Paper presented at the 68th annual meeting of the American Educational Research Association, New Orleans, LA. (ERIC Document Reproduction Service No. ED 249 043)

Herrnstein, R. J., & Murray, C. (1996). *The Bell curve: Intelligence and class structure in American life.* New York: Free Press.

Hiebert, E. H., & Raphael, T. E. (1996). Psychological perspectives on literacy and extensions to educational practice. In D. C. Berliner & R. C. Calfee (Eds.), *Handbook of educational psychology* (pp. 550–602). New York: Macmillan.

Hill, T., Lewicki, P., Czyzewska, M., & Schuller, G. (1990). The role of learned inferential encoding rules in the perception of faces: Effects of nonconscious self-perpetuation of a bias. *Journal of Experimental Social Psychology, 26*(4), 350–371.

Hill, T., Lewicki, P., & Neubauer, R. M. (1991). The development of depressive encoding dispositions: A case of self-perpetuation of biases. *Journal of Experimental Social Psychology, 27*(4), 392–409.

Hilton, J. L., & Von Hippel, W. (1996). Stereotypes. *Annual Review of Psychology, 47*, 237–271.

Hitt, M. A., Zikmund, W. G., & Pickens, B. A. (1982). Discrimination in industrial employment: An investigation of race and sex bias among professionals. *Work & Occupations, 9*(2), 217–231.

Hooper, H., & Walker, M. (2002). Makaton peer tutoring evaluation: 10 years on. *British Journal of Learning Disabilities, 30*(1), 38–42.

Horn, J. L. (2002). Selections of evidence, misleading assumptions, and oversimplifications: The political message of the Bell curve. In J. M. Fish (Ed.), *Race and intelligence: Separating science from myth* (pp. 297–325). Mahwah, NJ: Erlbaum.

Houle, N. (1992). Now, sure, I proud and can do everything. *Volta Review, 94*(4), 377–387.

Huba, M. E., & Freed, J. E. (2000). *Learner-centered assessment on college campuses: Shifting the focus from teaching to learning.* Boston: Allyn & Bacon.

Hudson, J. B., & Hines-Hudson, B. M. (1999). A study of the contemporary racial attitudes of Whites and African Americans. *Western Journal of Black Studies, 23*(1), 22–34.

Hunter, J., Yule, W., Urbanowicz, M. A., & Lansdown, R. (1989). Cross-validation of short forms of the WISC–R in two British samples. *British Journal of Educational Psychology, 59*(3), 366–371.

Hurwitz, J., & Peffley, M. (1997). Public perceptions of race and crime: The role of racial stereotypes. *American Journal of Political Science, 41*(2), 375–402.

Hutchinson, E. O. (1997, December 18). Perspectives on race: Conservatives need to face facts. *The Los Angeles Times,* p. B9.

Igou, F. P. (2001). An empirical examination of the impact of banding and rank order methods of selection test score use on race and utility. *Dissertation Abstracts International, 62,* 6B, p. 2982.

Ingraham, L. A. (1995). Women do not need affirmative action. In A. E. Sadler (Ed.), *Affirmative action* (pp. 66–69). San Diego, CA: Greenhaven.

Insko, C. A., Nacoste, R. W., & Moe, J. L. (1983). Belief congruence and racial discrimination: Review of the evidence and critical evaluation. *European Journal of Social Psychology, 13*(2), 153–174.

Jackson, J. L. (1995). People of color need affirmative action. In A. E. Sadler (Ed.), *Affirmative action* (pp. 8–13). San Diego, CA: Greenhaven.

Jacobson, M. B., & Koch, W. (1977). Women as leaders: Performance evaluation as a function of method of leader selection. *Organizational Behavior & Human Decision Processes, 20*(1), 149–157.

James, E. H., Brief, A. P., Dietz, J. C., & Cohen, R. (2001). Prejudice matters: Understanding the reactions of Whites to affirmative action programs targeted to benefit Blacks. *Journal of Applied Psychology, 86*(6), 1120–1128.

Jencks, C., & Phillips, M. (1998). *The black–white test score gap.* Washington, DC: Brookings Institution Press.

Jensen, A. R. (1998). *The g factor: The science of mental ability.* Westport, CT: Praeger.

Johnson, D. W., & Johnson, R. T. (1990). Cooperative learning and achievement. In S. Shlomo (Ed.), *Cooperative learning: Theory and research* (pp. 23–37). New York: Praeger.

Johnson, D. W., Johnson, R. T., & Taylor, B. (1993). Impact of cooperative and individualistic learning on high-ability students' achievement, self-esteem, and social acceptance. *Journal of Social Psychology, 133*(6), 839–844.

Kahlenberg, R. D. (1997). The remedy: Class, race, and affirmative action by HarperCollins (paper). ISBN: 046509824X. Rpt. ed.

Kane, T. J. (1998). Racial and ethnic preferences in college admissions. In C. Jencks & M. Phillips (Eds.), *The black-white test score gap* (pp. 431–456). Washington, DC: Brookings Institution Press.

Kasser, T., & Ryan, R. M. (2001). Be careful what you wish for: Optimal functioning and the relative attainment of intrinsic and extrinsic goals. In P. Schmuck & K. M. Sheldon (Eds.), *Life goals and well-being: Towards a positive psychology of human striving* (pp. 116–131). Seattle, WA: Hogrefe & Huber.

Katz, D., & Braly, K. (1933). Racial stereotypes in one hundred college students. *Journal of Abnormal and Social Psychology, 28,* 280–290.

Kidder, W. C. (2001). Does the LSAT mirror or magnify racial and ethnic differences in educational attainment? A study of equally achieving "elite" college students. *California Law Review, 89*(4), 1055.

King, C. M., & Johnson, L. M. (1999). Constructing meaning via reciprocal teaching. *Parent, Reading Research & Instruction, 38*(3), 169–186.

Kohn, A. (1993). *Punished by rewards: The trouble with gold stars, incentive plans, A's, praise, and other bribes.* Boston: Houghton Mifflin

Kohn, A. (1999). *The schools our children deserve: Moving beyond traditional classrooms and "tougher standards."* Boston: Houghton Mifflin.

Kohn, A. (2000). *The case against standardized testing: Raising the scores, ruining the schools.* Portsmouth, NH: Heinemann.

Kramer, R. A., Allen, L., & Gergen, P. J. (1995). Health and social characteristics and children's cognitive functioning: Results from a national cohort. *American Journal of Public Health, 85*(3), 312–318.

Kravitz, D. A., Harrison, D. A., Turner, M. E., Levine, E. L., Brannick, M. T., Denning, D. L., Russell, C. J., Conard, M. A., & Bhagat, R. S. (1996). *Affirmative action: A review of psychological and behavioral research.* Prepared by a subcommittee of the Scientific Affairs Committee of the Society for Industrial and Organizational Psychology. Bowling Green, OH: Society for Industrial and Organizational Psychology.

Krudwig, K. M. (2000, April). *Relating teacher's pedagogical beliefs to their classroom actions.* Paper presented at the annual conference of the American Educational Research Association, New Orleans, LA.

Kruglanski, A. W., & Webster, D. M. (1996). Motivated closing of the mind: "Seizing" and "freezing." *Psychological Review, 103*(2), 263–283.

Kulatunga-Moruzi, C., & Norman, G. R. (2002). Validity of admissions measures in predicting performance outcomes: The contribution of cognitive and non-cognitive dimensions. *Teaching & Learning in Medicine, 14*(1), 34–42.

Laird, B. (2002, May 17). Bending admissions to political ends. *Chronicle of Higher Education, 48*(36), p. B11.

Lamm, Z. (1976). Conflicting theories of instruction: Conceptual dimension. Berkeley, CA: McCutchan.

Lawlor, S., Richman, S., & Richman, C. L. (1997). The validity of using the SAT as a criterion for black and white students' admission to college. *College Student Journal, 31*(4), 507–515.

Ledvinka, J., & Scarpello, V. G. (1991). *Federal regulation of personnel and human resource management.* Boston: PWS-Kent.

Lee, K., & Lodewijks, H. G. L. C. (1995). The adaptation of international students' learning styles to different learning contexts. *College Student Journal, 29*(3), 319–332.

Lee, Y., Ottati, V., & Hussain, I. (2001). Attitudes toward "illegal" immigration into the United States: California Proposition 187. *Hispanic Journal of Behavioral Sciences, 23*(4), 430–443.

Lemann, N. (1999, November). The reading wars: Political dispute over reading education methods. *The Atlantic Monthly, 280*(5), 128–133.

Leonard, J. S. (1984). Antidiscrimination or reverse discrimination: The impact of changing demographics, Title VII, and affirmative action on productivity. *The Journal of Human Resources, 19,* 145–174.

Lepore, L., & Brown, R. (1997). Category and stereotype activation: Is prejudice inevitable? *Journal of Personality & Social Psychology, 72*(2), 275–287.

Levin, B. (1994, April 4–8). *Improving education productivity through a focus on learners.* Paper presented at the annual meeting of the American Educational Research Association, New Orleans, LA.

Lippman, W. (1922). *Public opinion.* New York: Harcourt Brace Jovanovich.

Little, B. L., Murry, W. D., & Wimbush, J. C. (1998). Perceptions of workplace affirmative action plans: A psychological perspective. *Group & Organization Management, 23*(1), 27–47.

Liu, G. (2002, April 14). The myth and math of affirmative action. *The Washington Post,* p. B1.

Lively, K. (1995, July 28). University of California ends race-based hirings, admissions. *Chronicle of Higher Education.* Available: http://www.chronicle.com

Long, J. (2002). Symbolic reality bites: Women and racial/ethnic minorities in modern film. *Sociological Spectrum, 22*(3), 299–335.

Lott, B., & Maluso, D. (1995). Introduction: Framing the questions. In B. Lott & D. Maluso (Eds.), *The social psychology of interpersonal discrimination* (pp. 1–11). New York: Guilford Press.

Lynn, R., & Mau, W. C. (2001). Ethnic and sex differences in the predictive validity of the Scholastic Achievement Test for college grades. *Psychological Reports, 88*(3), pt. 2, 1099–1104.

Maio, G. R., & Esses, V. M. (1998). The social consequences of affirmative action: Deleterious effects on perceptions of groups. *Personality & Social Psychology Bulletin, 24*(1), 65–74.

Major, B., Feinstein, J., & Crocker, J. (1994). Attributional ambiguity of affirmative action. [Special issue]. *US Basic & Applied Social Psychology, 15*(1–2), 113–141.

Makri-Botsari, E. (2001). Causal links between academic intrinsic motivation, self-esteem, and unconditional acceptance by teachers in high school students. In R. J. Riding & S. G. Rayner (Eds.), *Self perception: International perspectives on individual differences* (Vol. 2) (pp. 209–220). Westport, CT: Ablex.

Maluso, D. (1995). Shaking hands with a clenched fist: Interpersonal racism. In B. Lott & D. Maluso (Eds.), *The social psychology of interpersonal discrimination* (pp. 50–79). New York: Guilford Press.

Matthews, D. R., & McLaughlin, T. F. (1995). Effects of learner-centered laboratory activities on achievement and students' preferences in two high school biology courses. *Perceptual & Motor Skills, 78*(1), 285–286.

Mayer, R. E. (1996). Learners as information processors: Legacies and limitations of educational psychology's second metaphor. [Special issue]. *Educational Psychologist, 31*(3–4), 151–161.

Mayo, M. W., & Christenfeld, N. (1999). Gender, race, and performance expectations of college students. *Journal of Multicultural Counseling & Development, 27*(2), 93–104.

McCombs, B. L. (2001). Preparing teachers to meet the needs of diverse learners in urban schools: The learner-centered framework. Seattle, WA: American Education Research Association. (ERIC Document Reproduction Service No. ED 461 705)

McCombs, B. L., & Whisler, J. S. (1997). *The learner-centered classroom and school.* San Francisco, CA: Jossey-Bass.

McConahay, J. B. (1983). Modern racism and modern discrimination: The effects of race, racial attitudes, and context on simulated hiring decisions. *Personality & Social Psychology Bulletin, 9*(4), 551–558.

McRae, M. B. (1991). Sex and race bias in employment decisions: Black women considered. *Journal of Employment Counseling, 28*(3), 91–98.

Meece, J. L., Blumenfeld, P. C., & Hoyle, R. H. (1988). Students' goal orientations and cognitive engagement in classroom activities. *Journal of Educational Psychology, 80*(4), 514–523.

Melear, C. T., & Alcock, M. W. (1998). *Learning styles and personality types of African American children: Implications for science education.* Paper presented at the annual meeting of the National Association for Research in Science Teaching, San Diego, CA. (ERIC Document Reproduction Service No. ED 418 874)

Menchaca, M. (1997). Early racist discourses: Roots of deficit thinking. In R. R. Valencia (Ed.), *The evolution of deficit thinking: Educational thought and practice* (pp. 13–40). London: Falmer Press.

Merritt, J. (2002, March 11). Wanted: A campus that looks like America. *Business Week*, p. 56.

Milbank, D. (2002, July 3). To revive agenda, Bush courts blacks; support sought for welfare reform, "faith-based" charity, homeownership. *The Washington Post*, p. A8.

Mintrom, M. (1993). Why efforts to equalize school funding have failed: Towards a positive theory. *Political Research Quarterly, 46*(4), 847–863.

Moss, P., & Tilly, C. (1996). "Soft" skills and race: An investigation of Black men's employment problems. *Work & Occupations, 23*(3), 252–276.

Muller, C., & Schiller, K. S. (2000). Leveling the playing field? Students' educational attainment and states' performance testing. *Sociology of Education, 73*(3), 196–218.

Murrell, A. J., & Jones, R. (1996). Assessing affirmative action: Past, present, and future. [Special issue]. *Journal of Social Issues, 52*(4), 77–92.

Nacoste, R. W., & Arbor, A. (1985). Selection procedure and responses to affirmative action: The case of favorable treatment. *Law & Human Behavior, 9*(3), 225–242.

Nacoste, R. W., & Lehman, D. (1987). Procedural stigma. [Special issue]. *Representative Research in Social Psychology, 17*(1), 25–38.

Neisser, U. (1998). *The rising curve: Long-term gains in IQ and related measures.* Washington, DC: American Psychological Association.

Nellen, T. (2001). The school-to-career web. Available: http://www.tnellen. com/ted/tc/stw. html

Nelson-Le Gall, S., & Jones, E. (1990). Cognitive-motivational influences on the task-related help-seeking behavior of Black children. *Child Development, 61*(2), 581–589.

Nichols, B. (2001, May 29). Expectations shadow Powell in Africa. *USA Today*, p. 7A.

Ogbu, J. U. (2002). Cultural amplifiers of intelligence: IQ and minority status in cross-cultural perspective. In J. M. Fish (Ed.), *Race and intelligence: Separating science from myth* (pp. 241–278). Mahwah, NJ: Erlbaum.

Ovando, M. N., & Alford, B. J. (1997, February 14–17). *Creating a culture of detracking in a learner-centered school: Issues, problems, and possibilities.* Paper presented at the 129th annual meeting of the American Association of School Administrators, Orlando, FL. (ERIC Document Reproduction Service No. ED 407 744)

Page, S. (2001). The CEIC Review, 2001. *CEIC Review, 10*(1–6).

Parker, C. P., Christiansen, N. D., & Baltes, B. B. (1997). Support for affirmative action, justice perceptions, and work attitudes: A study of gender and racial-ethnic group differences. *Journal of Applied Psychology, 82*(3), 376–389.

Parloff, R. (2002). Bakke to the future: Powell's artful fudge deserves more respect. *American Lawyer, 24*(2), 122–124.

Patterson, O. (1998). Is affirmative action on the way out? Should it be? A symposium. *Commentary, 105*(3), 43–46.

Pearl, A. (1997). Democratic education as an alternative to deficit thinking. In R. R. Valencia (Ed.), *The evolution of deficit thinking: Educational thought and practice. The Stanford series on education and public policy* (pp. 211–241). London: Falmer Press.

Peffley, M. (1994, July). The political impact of racial stereotypes in the United States. Invited paper presented at the Second International Congress on Prejudice, Discrimination, and Conflict, Jerusalem, Israel.

Peffley, M., & Hurwitz, J. (1998). Whites' stereotypes of Blacks: Sources and political consequences. In J. Hurwitz and M. Peffley (Eds.), *Perception and prejudice: Race and politics in the United States* (pp. 58–99). New Haven, CT: Yale University Press.

Perry, K. E. (1999). The role of learner-centered teaching practices in children's adjustment during the transition to elementary school. *Dissertation Abstracts International Section, 60,* 5A, p. 1451.

Picou, A., Gatlin-Watts, R., & Packer, J. (1998). A test for learning style differences for the U.S. border population. *Texas Papers in Foreign Language Education, 3*(2), 105–121.

Pigott, R. L., & Cowen, E. L. (2000). Teacher race, child race, racial congruence, and teacher ratings of children's school adjustment. *Journal of School Psychology, 38*(2), 177–195.

Pintrich, P. R., & De Groot, E. V. (1990). Motivational and self-regulated learning components of classroom academic performance. *Journal of Educational Psychology, 82,* 33–40.

Plous, S. (1996). Ten myths about affirmative action. *Journal of Social Issues, 52*(4), 25–31.

Pollard, K. M., & O'Hare, W. P. (1999). Income, wealth, and poverty. *Population Bulletin, 54*(3), 34–41.

Pratkanis, A. R., & Turner, M. E. (1996). The proactive removal of discriminatory barriers: affirmative action as effective help. [Special issue]. *Journal of Social Issues, 52*(4), 111–133.

Pratkanis, A. R., Turner, M. E., & Malos, S. B. (2002). Toward a resolution of an American tension: Some applications of the helping model of affirmative action to schooling. In J. Aronson (Ed.), *Improving academic achievement: Impact of psychological factors on education* (pp. 329–361). San Diego, CA: Academic Press.

Puddington, A. (1995). Affirmative action should be eliminated. In A. E. Sadler (Ed.), *Affirmative action* (pp. 70–83). San Diego, CA: Greenhaven.

Pugh, G. M., & Boer, D. P. (1991). Normative data on the validity of Canadian substitute items for the WAIS–R Information subtest. *Canadian Journal of Behavioral Science, 23*(2), 149–158.

Pugh, K. J. (2002). Teaching for transformative experiences in science: An investigation of the effectiveness of two instructional elements. *Teachers College Record, 104*(6), 1101–1137.

Rallis, S. F. (1996). Creating learner centered schools: Dreams and practices. *Educational Horizons, 75*(1), 20–26.

Reibstein, L. (1998, January 5). What color is an A? *Newsweek, 131,* 76.

Reifman, A. (2000). Revisiting the Bell curve. *Psycoloquy,* 11, n.p.

Rhode, D. L. (1997). Affirmative action. *National Forum, 77*(2), 12–17.

Richardson, E. H. (1981). Cultural and historical perspectives in counseling American Indians. In D. W. Sue (Ed.), *Counseling the culturally different* (pp. 225–227). New York: Wiley.

Roberts, S. (1995, June 18). Moving on up; the greening of America's black middle class. *The New York Times*, sec. 4, p. 1.

Robinson, R. K., Seydel, J., & Douglas, C. (1998). Affirmative action: The facts, the myths, and the future. *Employee Responsibilities & Rights Journal, 11*(2), 99–115.

Rokeach, M., Smith, P., & Evans, R. (1960). Two kinds of prejudice or one? In M. Rokeach (Ed.), *The open and the closed mind* (pp. 132–168). New York: Basic Books.

Roscigno, V. J., & Ainsworth-Darnell, J. W. (1999). Race, cultural capital, and educational resources: Persistent inequalities and achievement returns. *Sociology of Education, 72*(3), 158–160.

Roth, J., & Damico, S. B. (1999). Student perspectives on learning and instruction: Differences by race/ethnicity and gender. *Journal of At-Risk Issues, 6*(1), 32–39.

Rubio, P. F. (2001). *A history of affirmative action, 1619–2000.* Jackson: University Press of Mississippi.

Sackett, P. R. (1996a). Interpreting the ban on minority group score adjustment in preemployment testing. In R. S. Barrett (Ed.), *Fair employment strategies in human resource management* (pp. 246–256). Westport, CT: Quorum Books.

Sackett, P. R. (1996b). Multi-stage selection strategies: A Monte Carlo investigation of effects on performance and minority hiring. *Personnel Psychology, 49*(3), 549–572.

Sackett, P. R., & Roth, L. (1991). A Monte Carlo examination of banding and rank order methods of test score use in personnel selection. *Human Performance, 4*(4), 279–295.

Sackett, P. R., & Wilk, S. L. (1994). Within-group norming and other forms of score adjustment in preemployment testing. *American Psychologist, 49*(11), 929–954.

Saegert, S., Swap, W., & Zajonc, R. (1973). Exposure, context, and interpersonal attraction. *Journal of Personality & Social Psychology, 25*(2), 234–242.

Salinas, M. F., & Aronson, J. (2002). *Why do Latinos underperform? Motivation, anxiety, and stereotype threat.* Manuscript submitted for publication.

Salisbury-Glennon, J. D., Gorrell, J., Sanders, S., Boyd, P., & Kamen, M. (1999, April 19–23). Self-regulated learning strategies used by the learners in a learner-centered school. Paper presented at the annual meeting of the American Educational Research Association, Montreal, Quebec, Canada. (ERIC Document Reproduction Service No. ED 434 944)

Sbarra, D. A., & Pianta, R. C. (2001). Teacher ratings of behavior among African American and caucasian children during the first two years of school. *Psychology in the Schools, 38*(3), 229–238.

Schmidt, F. L., & Hunter, J. E. (1995). The fatal internal contradiction in banding: Its statistical rationale is logically inconsistent with its operational procedures. *Human Performance, 8*(3), 203–214.

Schmitt, A. P., & Dorans, N. J. (1991). Factors related to differential item functioning for Hispanic examinees on the Scholastic Aptitude Test. In G. D. Keller & J. R. Deneen (Eds.), *Assessment and access: Hispanics in higher education* (pp. 105–132). Albany: State University of New York Press.

Schrag, P. (1997, January–February). When preferences disappear. *American Prospect, 30* , 38(4).

Schrag, P. (2002, May 6). War on the SAT. *American Prospect, 13*(8), 24(4)

Schrenko, L. (1994). *Structuring a learner-centered school.* Arlington Heights, IL: IRI Skylight.

Schuh, K. (2001). Exploring the connections: Knowledge construction in the learner-centered classroom. *Dissertation Abstracts International, 61,* 7A, p. 2598.

Sewell, T. E., DuCette, J. P., & Shapiro, J. P. (1998). Educational assessment and diversity. In N. M. Lambert & B. L. McCombs (Eds.), *How stu-*

dents learn: Reforming schools through learner-centered education (pp. 311–338). Washington, DC: American Psychological Association.

Shade, B. J. R. (1997). *Culture, style, and the educative process: Making schools work for racially diverse students* (2nd ed.). Springfield, IL: Thomas.

Shaull, R. (1970). Introduction. *Pedagogy of the oppressed* by Paulo Freire. Trans. Myra Bergman Ramos. New York: Herder & Herder.

Sherif, M. (1967). *Social interaction: Process and products.* Chicago: Aldine.

Sigelman, L. (1997). The public and disadvantage-based affirmative action: An early assessment. *Social Science Quarterly, 78*(4), 1011–1022.

Sigelman, L., & Tuch, S. A. (1997). Meta stereotypes: Blacks' perceptions of Whites' stereotypes of Blacks. *Public Opinion Quarterly, 61*(1), 87–101.

Silva, J. M., & Jacobs, R. R. (1993). Performance as a function of increased minority hiring. *Journal of Applied Psychology, 78*(4), 591–601.

Simpson, A., & Strong, S. R. (1986). Effects of prejudice and power on influence and attribution. *Journal of Social & Clinical Psychology, 4*(4), 423–432.

Skrentny, J. D. (1996). *The ironies of affirmative action: Politics, culture, and justice in America.* Chicago: University of Chicago Press.

Slavin, R. E., & Cooper, R. (1999). Improving intergroup relations: Lessons learned from cooperative learning programs. *Journal of Social Issues, 55*(4), 647–663.

Smith, G. P. (1998). *Common sense about uncommon knowledge: the knowledge bases for diversity* (Report No. BBB14763). Washington, DC: American Association of Colleges for Teacher Education. (ERIC Document Reproduction Service No. ED 417 153)

Smith, H. P., & Rosen, E. W. (1958). Some psychological correlates of world mindedness and authoritarism. *Journal of Personality, 26,* 170–183.

Smith, T. W. (1991). *Ethnic images in the United States.* Washington, DC: The Polling Report.

Smith, T. W. (2001). *Intergroup relations in a diverse America.* Chicago: National Opinion Research Center.

Spencer, S. J. (1994). *The effect of stereotype vulnerability on women's math performance.* Unpublished doctoral dissertation, University of Michigan, Ann Arbor.

Spencer, S. J., Steele, C. M., & Brown, D. M. (1997). *Stereotype vulnerability and women's math performance.* Unpublished manuscript, University of Waterloo.

Steeh, C., & Krysan, M. (1996). Affirmative action and the public, 1970–1995. *Public Opinion Quarterly, 60*(1), 128–159.

Steel, B. S., & Lovrich, N. P. (1987). Equality and efficiency tradeoffs in affirmative action—Real or imagined? The case of women in policing. *The Social Science Journal, 24*(1), 53–70.

Steele, C., & Aronson, J. (1995). Stereotype threat and the intellectual test performance of African Americans. *Journal of Personality & Social Psychology, 69*(5), 797–811.

Steele, C. M. (1997). A threat in the air: How stereotypes shape intellectual identity and performance. *American Psychologist, 52*(6), 613–629.

Steele, S. (1998). *Dream deferred: The second betrayal of black America.* New York: HarperCollins.

Stephan, W. G. (1985). Intergroup Relations. In G. Lindzey & E. Aronson (Eds.), *The handbook of social psychology* (Vol. 2) (pp. 599–658). New York: Random House.

Stephenson, P., & Warwick, P. (2001). Peer tutoring in the primary science classroom. *Investigating, 17*(2), 11–13.

Sternberg, R. J. (1994). Allowing for thinking styles. *Educational Leadership, 52*(3), 36–40.

Stewart, L. D., & Perlow, R. (2001). Applicant race, job status, and racial attitude as predictors of employment discrimination. *Journal of Business & Psychology, 16*(2), 259–275.

Stewart, M. M., & Shapiro, D. L. (2000). Selection based on merit versus demography: Implications across race and gender lines. *Journal of Applied Psychology, 85*(2), 219–231.

Stricker, L., Rock, D., Pollack, J., & Wenglinsky, H. (2002). *Measuring educational disadvantage of SAT candidates.* College Board Research Report No. 2002-1. Princeton, NJ: Educational Testing Service.

Stroebe, W., & Insko, C. A. (1989). Stereotype, prejudice and discrimination: Changing conceptions in theory and research. In D. Bar-Tal, C. F. Graumann, A. W. Kruglanski, & W. Stroebe (Eds.), *Stereotyping and prejudice: Changing conceptions* (pp. 3–34). Berlin, Germany: Springer.

Summers, R. J. (1991). The influence of affirmative action on perceptions of a beneficiary's qualifications. *Journal of Applied Social Psychology, 21*(15), 1265–1276.

Suzuki, L. A., & Valencia, R. R. (1997). Race-ethnicity and measured intelligence: Educational implications. [Special issue]. *American Psychologist, 52*(10), 1103–1114.

Swift, P. (1998, January 31). Is racial politics the force behind welfare reform? *The Buffalo News,* p. 7C.

Symonds, W. C. (2002, October 14). CLOSING THE SCHOOL GAP, If no child is to be left behind, we must overhaul funding. *Business Week,* p. 124.

Tajfel, H. (1970). Experiments in intergroup discrimination. *Scientific American, 223*(2), 96–102.

Tajfel, H. (1982). Social psychology of intergroup attitudes. *Annual Review of Psychology, 33*, 1–39.

Tajfel, H., & Turner, J. (1979). An integrative theory of intergroup conflict. In W. Austin & S. Worchel (Eds.), *The social psychology of intergorup relations* (pp. 33–47). Monterrey, CA: Brooks-Cole.

Tal-Or, N., Boninger, D., & Gleicher, F. (2002). Understanding the conditions and processes necessary for intergroup contact to reduce prejudice. In G. Salomon & B. Nevo (Eds.), *Peace education: The concept, principles, and practices around the world* (pp. 89–107). Mahwah, NJ: Erlbaum.

Tan, A., Fujioka, Y., & Tan, G. (2000). Television use, stereotypes of African Americans and opinions on affirmative action: An affective model of policy reasoning. *Communication Monographs, 67*(4), 362–371.

Taylor, M. C. (1994). Impact of affirmative action on beneficiary groups: Evidence from the 1990 General Social Survey. [Special issue]. *Basic & Applied Social Psychology, 15*(1–2), 143–178.

Taylor-Carter, M. A., Doverspike, D., & Cook, K. D. (1996). The effects of affirmative action on the female beneficiary. *US Human Resource Development Quarterly, 7*(1), 31–54.

Tedin, K. L. (1994). Self-interest, symbolic values, and the financial equalization of the public schools. *The Journal of Politics, 56*(3), 628–650.

Thornton, L. J., & McEntee, M. E. (1995). Learner centered schools as a mindset, and the connection with mindfulness and multiculturalism. *Theory Into Practice, 34*(4), 250–257.

Tomkiewicz, J., Brenner, O. C., & Adeyemi-Bello, T. (1998). The impact of perceptions and stereotypes on the managerial mobility of African Americans. *Journal of Social Psychology, 138*(1), 88–92.

Traver, H. A. (1999). Evaluations and attributions of beneficiaries and non-beneficiaries of affirmative action in mental and physical tasks. *Dissertation Abstracts International, 60*, 3B, p. 1340.

The trouble with Susan Smith. (1995, July 15). *The Economist*, p. 22.

Truax, K., Cordova, D. I., Wood, A., Wright, E., Crosby, F., Swim, J. K., & Stangor, C. (Eds.). (1998). Undermined? Affirmative action from the target's point of view. *Prejudice: The target's perspective* (pp. 171–188). San Diego, CA: Academic Press.

Turner, M. E., & Pratkanis, A. R. (1994). Affirmative action as help: A review of recipient reactions to preferential selection and affirmative action. [Special issue]. *Basic & Applied Social Psychology, 15*(1–2), 43–69.

Udvari-Solner, A., & Thousand, J. S. (1996). Creating a responsive curriculum for inclusive schools. *Remedial & Special Education, 17*(3), 182–192.

U.S. Census Bureau. (2001). *Poverty in the United States: 2000*. Current Population Reports, Series P60-214. Washington, DC. U.S. Government Printing Office.

The U.S.: Racial stereotypes persist in US, study finds. (1991, January 10). *The Christian Science Monitor,* p. 6.

U.S. Department of Labor (USDOL). (1971). Revised Order No. 4. (41 CFR 60-2. 24(e)).

Valencia, R. R. (1997). *The evolution of deficit thinking: Educational thought and practice*. London: Falmer Press.

Valencia, R. R., & Salinas, M. F. (2000). Test bias. In R. R. Valencia & L. Suzuki (Eds.), *Intelligence testing and minority students*. New York: Sage.

Valencia, R. R., & Suzuki, L. A. (2001). *Intelligence testing and minority students: Foundations, performance factors, and assessment issues*. Thousand Oaks, CA: Sage.

Valencia, R. R., Villareal, B., & Salinas, M. F. (2002). Cultural bias in intelligence testing for Mexican Americans. In R. R. Valencia (Ed.), *Chicano school failure and success* (2nd ed.). London: Falmer Press.

Vallerand, R. J., & Bissonnette, R. (1992). Intrinsic, extrinsic, and amotivational styles as predictors of behavior: A prospective study. *Journal of Personality, 60*(3), 599–620.

Vallerand, R. J., Fortier, M. S., & Guay, F. (1997). Self-determination and persistence in a real-life setting: Toward a motivational model of high school dropout. *Journal of Personality & Social Psychology, 72*(5), 1161–1176.

Vars, F. E., & Bowen, W. G. (1998). Scholastic Aptitude Test scores, race, and academic performance in selective colleges and universities. In C. Jencks & M. Phillips (Eds.), *The black–white test score gap* (pp. 457–479). Washington, DC: Brookings Institution Press.

Webb, C. T., Waugh F. E., & Herbert J. D. (1993). Relationship between locus of control and performance on the National Board of Medical Examiners, part 1, among black medical students. *Psychological Reports, 72*(3), 1171–1177.

Weber, R., & Crocker, J. (1983). Cognitive processes in the revision of stereotypic beliefs. *Journal of Personality & Social Psychology, 45*(5), 961–977.

White House. (1995, July 19). Affirmative Action Review: Report to the president. Available: http://clinton1. nara. gov/White_House/EOP/OP/html/aa/aa-index. html

Whitworth, R. H., & Barrientos, G. A. (1990). Comparison of Hispanic and Anglo Graduate Record Examination scores and academic performance. *Journal of Psychoeducational Assessment, 8*(2), 128–132.

Wightman, L. F. (1997). The threat to diversity in legal education: An empirical analysis of the consequences of abandoning race as a factor in law school admission decisions. *New York University Law Review, 72*(1), 1–53.

Williams, D. R., Jackson, J. S., Brown, T. N., Torres, M., Forman, T. A., & Brown, K. (1999). Traditional and contemporary prejudice and urban whites' support for affirmative action and government help. *Social Problems, 46*(4), 503–527.

Wilson, R. (1998). Affirmative action: Yesterday, today and beyond. In S. N. Colamery (Ed.), *Affirmative action: Catalyst or albatross?* (pp. 10–33). Commack, NY: Nova.

Witt, S. L. (1990). Affirmative action and job satisfaction: Self-interested v. public spirited perspectives on social equity—Some sobering findings from the academic workplace. *Review of Public Personnel Administration, 10*, 73–93.

Zajonc, R. B. (1968). Attitudinal effects of mere exposure. *Journal of Personality and Social Psychology, 9*(Monograph Suppl. 2, pt. 2).

Zedeck, S., Cascio, W. F., & Goldstein, I. L. (1996). Sliding bands: An alternative to top-down selection. In R. S. Barrett (Ed.), *Fair employment strategies in human resource management* (pp. 222–234). Westport, CT: Quorum Books.

Zimmerman, B. J. (1994). Dimensions of academic self-regulation: A conceptual framework for education. In D. H. Schunk & B. Zimmerman (Eds.), *Self-regulation of learning and performance: Issues and educational applications*. Hillsdale, NJ: Erlbaum.

Zogby International. (2001, March 6). *Teenagers and entertainment stereotyping poll*. Available: http://www.zogby.com/news/ReadNews.dbm? ID=348

Zsolnai, A. (2002). Relationship between children's social competence, learning motivation, and school achievement. *Educational Psychology, 22*(3), 317–330.

Further Reading

Bernadette, M., Masten, W. G., & Huang, J. (1999). Differences between African American and Caucasian students on critical thinking and learning style. *College Student Journal, 33*(4), 538–542.

Buckley, W. F., Jr. (1994, December 19). Is everybody a racist? Public perceptions about race and crime. *National Review, 46*(24), 71.

Butler, R., & Nisan, M. (1986). Effects of no feedback, task-related comments, and grades on intrinsic motivation and performance. *Journal of Educational Psychology, 78*(3), 210–216.

Carroll, J. B. (1997). Theoretical and technical issues in identifying a factor of general intelligence. In B. Devlin, S. E., Fienberg, D. P. Resnick, & K. Roeder (Eds.), *Intelligence genes and success: Scientists respond to the Bell curve* (pp. 125–156). New York: Springer-Verlag.

Cavallo, A., El-Abbadi, H., & Heeb, R. (1997). The hidden gender restriction: The need for proper controls when testing for racial discrimination. In B. Devlin, S. E. Fienberg, D. P. Resnick, & K. Roeder (Eds.), *Intelligence genes and success: Scientists respond to the Bell curve* (pp. 193–215). New York: Springer-Verlag.

Cawley, J., Conneely, K., Heckman, J., & Vytlacil, E. (1997). Cognitive ability wages and meritocracy. In B. Devlin, S. E. Fienberg, D. P. Resnick, & K. Roeder (Eds.), *Intelligence genes and success: Scientists respond to the Bell curve* (pp. 179–192). New York: Springer-Verlag.

Daniels, M., Devlin, B., & Roeder, K. (1997). Of genes and IQ. In B. Devlin, S. E. Fienberg, D. P. Resnick, & K. Roeder (Eds.), *Intelligence genes and success: Scientists respond to the Bell curve* (pp. 45–70). New York: Springer-Verlag.

Devlin, B., Fienberg, S. E., Resnick, D. P., & Roeder, K. (Eds.). (1997). *Intelligence genes and success: Scientists respond to the Bell curve*. New York: Springer-Verlag.

Dorsey, M. S., & Jackson, A. P. (1995). Afro-American students' perceptions of factors affecting academic performance at a predominantly White school. *Western Journal of Black Studies, 19*(3), 189–195.

Fischer, C. S., Hout, M., Jankowski, M. S., Lucas, S. R., Swidler, A., & Voss, K. (1996). *Inequality by design: Cracking the Bell curve myth*. Princeton, NJ: Princeton University Press.

Flink, C., Boggiano, A. K., & Main, D. S. (1992). Children's achievement-related behaviors: The role of extrinsic and intrinsic motivational orientations. In A. K. Boggiano & T. S. Pittman (Eds.), *Achievement and motivation: A social-developmental perspective* (pp. 189–214). Cambridge, UK: Cambridge University Press.

Flynn, J. R. (1987). Massive IQ gains in 14 nations: What IQ tests really measure. *Psychological Bulletin, 101,* 171–191.

Glymour, C. (1997). Social statistics and genuine inquiry: Reflections on the Bell curve. In B. Devlin, S. E. Fienberg, D. P. Resnick, & K. Roeder (Eds.), *Intelligence genes and success: Scientists respond to the Bell curve* (pp. 257–280). New York: Springer-Verlag.

Gould, S. J. (1996). *The mismeasure of man* (Rev. and exp. ed.). New York: Norton.

Graumann, C. F., & Wintermantel, M. (1989). Discriminatory speech acts: A functional approach. In D. Bar-Tal, C. F. Graumann, A. W. Kruglanski, & W. Stroebe (Eds.), *Stereotyping and prejudice: Changing conceptions* (pp. 183–204). Berlin, Germany: Springer.

Hamilton, D. L., & Sherman, S. J. (1989). Illusory correlations: Implications for stereotype theory and research. In D. Bar-Tal, C. F. Graumann, A. W. Kruglanski, & W. Stroebe (Eds.), *Stereotyping and prejudice: Changing conceptions* (pp. 59–82). Berlin, Germany: Springer.

Hidi, S. (2000). *An interest researcher's perspective: The effects of extrinsic and intrinsic factors on motivation.* In C. Sansone & J. M. Harack-iewicz (Eds.), *Intrinsic and extrinsic motivation: The search for optimal motivation and performance* (pp. 309–339). San Diego, CA: Academic Press.

Holzer, H., & Neumark, D. (2000). Assessing affirmative action. *Journal of Economic Literature, 38*(3), 483–568.

Kwate, N., & Oyo, A. (2001). Intelligence or misorientation? Eurocentrism in the WISC-III. *Journal of Black Psychology, 27*(2), 221–238.

Mullen, B., & Johnson, C. (1990). Distinctiveness-based illusory correlations and stereotyping: A meta-analytic integration. *British Journal of Social Psychology, 29*(1), 11–27.

Okagaki, L., Frensch, P. A., & Dodson, N. E. (1996). Mexican American children's perceptions of self and school achievement. *Hispanic Journal of Behavioral Sciences, 18*(4), 469–484.

Simon, M. C., Repper, D. P., & Heilman, M. E. (1987). Intentionally favored, unintentionally harmed? Impact of sex-based preferential selection on self-perceptions and self-evaluations. *Journal of Applied Psychology, 72*(1), 62–68.

Stephan, W. G. (1977). Stereotyping: The roles of ingroup–outgroup differences in causal attribution for behavior. *Journal of Social Psychology, 101*(2), 255–266.

Tajfel, H., & Turner, J. (1985). The social identity theory of intergroup behavior. In S. Worchel & W. G. Austin (Eds.), *Psychology of intergroup relations* (pp. 7–24). Chicago: Nelson-Hall.

Tanaka, A., & Yamauchi, H. (2001). A model for achievement motives, goal orientations, intrinsic interest, and academic achievement. *Psychological Reports, 88*(1), 123–135.

Vincent, J., & Roscigno, J. W. (1999). Race, cultural capital, and educational resources: Persistent inequalities and achievement returns. *Ainsworth-Darnell Sociology of Education, 72*(3), 158–160.

Wong, M. M., & Csikszentmihalyi, M. (1991). Motivation and academic achievement: The effects of personality traits and the quality of experience. *Journal of Personality, 59*(3), 539–574.

Index

About the Author

MOISES F. SALINAS is Assistant Professor of Psychology at Central Connecticut State University.